21 YEARS GONE

JACK OSBOURNE

21 YEARS GONE
THE AUTOBIOGRAPHY

WITH ADAM PARFITT

MACMILLAN

First published 2006 by Macmillan
an imprint of Pan Macmillan Ltd
Pan Macmillan, 20 New Wharf Road, London N1 9RR
Basingstoke and Oxford
Associated companies throughout the world
www.panmacmillan.com

ISBN-13: 978-0-230-01432-9 (HB)
ISBN-10: 0-230-01432-1
ISBN-13: 978-0-230-01522-7 (TPB)
ISBN-10: 0-230-01522-0

3 5 7 9 8 6 4 2

A CIP catalogue record for this book is available from
the British Library.

Typeset by Intype London Ltd
Printed and bound in Great Britain by
Mackays of Chatham plc, Chatham, Kent

This book is for my family and friends.
You are all very special to me.

CONTENTS

PROLOGUE

EL CAPITAN, YOSEMITE VALLEY, CALIFORNIA
SEPTEMBER 2005

They say that if you fall to your death, you see your life flash before your eyes. If I fall now, it will take fifteen seconds to hit the ground. Sounds a lot, but I can't help wondering if that will be enough time.

I'm thousands of feet above sea level. A two-inch ledge and a rope are the only things that are stopping me from falling to earth. It's dark. The temperature is falling dangerously low. My muscles ache so much I can hardly move, and I hurt with hunger. I've been hanging here for hours. My companions are either hundreds of feet below or hundreds of feet above, and right now I don't know if I'm going to make it to the summit. I'm beginning to wonder what the hell I'm doing here. And I'm beginning to wonder, if I fall, which bits of my life I will see the most clearly.

To be honest, there are things that I don't much want to remember, but which I know I will never forget. Bent over a line of opiates and inhaling deeply, too fucked up to know where I am or what I'm doing. Begging my friends to give me a fix of heroin. Waking up in hotel rooms with blood on my face and empty pill and alcohol bottles scattered around. Vomiting in my sleep. Passing out in swimming pools and having to be rescued by friends only slightly less high than me. Being told my mum might die, and then trying to take my own life so that I wouldn't have to deal with it.

But I have to put those thoughts from my mind. When you're pushing yourself to the limit like this, you have to keep positive. Lose your concentration and you make mistakes. And mistakes kill people on El Capitan.

When I first set eyes on the sheer cliff face and was told that I would have to climb it in six months' time, I didn't think it was possible. Hardly anybody thought it was possible. Some of them even laughed at the suggestion. I don't blame them. After all, if I'd been told the same thing four years ago, I'd have been laughing with them. Climb El Capitan? What's the point? Why would I do that when I've got a refrigerator full of beers and a box full of pills? Where's the party to be had halfway up some fucking rock face?

To the world I was Jack Osbourne, TV celebrity. Funny Jack. Party Jack. Jack-the-lad. Some of them thought I was a bit arrogant, a bit whiny. Maybe they were right, but what the hell? They still kept tuning in. My face was on the front cover of magazines the world over. I got paid more money than most people can dream of just to be myself. Girls wanted my autograph. Some of them wanted more than that. No matter that I was a bit overweight. No matter that I liked the occasional drink. No matter that I smoked a joint now and then.

No matter that I was only fifteen years old. Life was good.

What would they have thought if they had known the truth? What would they have thought if they had known that beneath the jovial exterior was an insecure kid sub-consciously wincing from the glare of publicity? What would they have thought if they had known that I was a teenage alcoholic and a drug addict?

Would they have laughed quite so hard if the cameras had captured me at my lowest, crying into a pillow in the dead of night, begging a God I didn't believe in to end my life, and to end it now?

I have to push on. I have to find the energy from somewhere so that I can climb this mountain just as I have conquered the metaphorical ones that preceded it. Only then can I get back down to earth and revel in what I've achieved. At the foot of the mountain I know my parents will be waiting. Expectant. Proud. We will hug each other, and probably cry, knowing that what I have just achieved is more than a sporting endeavour. It will be a personal triumph, documentary proof that I'm not that arrogant, scared, lost little kid any more. Proof, to myself and everyone else, that I've put those demons behind me.

But it's been a long road. Ever since I was small, I've listened to my dad telling funny stories about his life. It's been quite a life, and the stories are good. But some-where in the back of my head, I always knew that I wanted my own stories to tell.

And now I have.

I've done things most people will never do, seen places most people will never see. And I'm a different Jack Osbourne to the one the public think they know.

Truth to tell, I'm a different Jack Osbourne to the one I've spent most of my life with . . .

ONE

THE KIDS ARE ALRIGHT

I hate it when I hear people say, 'You know, I've always felt different, even as a kid.' Every kid feels different – it goes with the territory – but to say so out loud sounds kind of insincere, like they've been spending a bit too much time analysing themselves. But if I had to be honest, looking back at my early childhood, it would be insincere of me *not* to say that growing up as the son of Ozzy and Sharon Osbourne was – how can I put it? – a bit out of the ordinary.

I don't want to give you the wrong idea. It's not like my dad was walking round the house biting the heads off bats and practising devil worship every morning before breakfast – the Prince of Darkness is just his professional title, and he tended not to bring his work home with him – but it is true that I remember going to my friends' houses on play days or for the weekend and thinking that everyone else's family seemed to be run along the same lines as each other. Everyone's, that is, except mine. Our family just *felt* different. Not normal. My friends' dads would be at home a lot; mine would be on tour for half the year. Their mums were, for the most part, housewives – looking after the kids, cooking meals, keeping the household running; my earliest memory of my mum was that she was always on the phone, taking care of business. The other stuff was done by a constantly changing army of nannies who tried to keep us all in line.

It wasn't just me, either. I was always aware that other kids around me knew that there was something different about us. They were too young to know what it was, I suppose, but there were always remarks, little comments about me and my family that they picked up from fuck knows where. 'Your dad's crazy.' 'Your dad's been to jail.' 'Your dad bites the heads off animals.' I heard it all and, as any kid would, I used to get upset by it. The man they were describing was not the man I knew, the man I looked up to and respected, as I still do. And I never really understood how people could know all that stuff. I knew he was a musician, a singer, and I suppose that somewhere in my consciousness I knew that he was famous, but I never really knew why anyone would be aware of all that other shit, or why they would be interested. To me, he was just my dad. Gentle. Funny. Attentive. Whenever he was around he'd be playing games with us, taking us for walks, reading us bedtime stories – although not being a great reader, he used to make them up as he went along, and they were always ten times better than the actual book. Sometimes he used to pretend to be asleep when we were all watching TV, only to jump up and scare the living daylights out of us when we least expected it. OK, so he was a little crazy, perhaps; maybe a bit too fond of a drink; but I adored him, like all little boys should adore their dad.

I was born on 8 November 1985, the youngest of three and brother to Kelly, who you've probably seen or heard, and Aimee, who you almost certainly haven't. Aimee was two years old when I was born, and Kelly was one, so we all arrived pretty close together. We were a tight-knit family – we still are – and the overwhelming impression I have of being a little kid is that I was perfectly happy and contented. Despite the fact that we lived in different circumstances to most other people, cocooned in the weird bubble of the Ozzy Osbourne show, Mum and Dad always went out of their way to make sure that we felt safe, cared for and above all loved. I never felt scared and I never felt threatened. Even when Dad's behaviour got a bit out of control, I remember taking it all in my stride.

Beel House, where I lived for the first five or six years of my life, was a kids' paradise. My first home, in fact, had been in Hampstead, but we soon moved into this gorgeous Georgian residence nestled away in a quiet corner of the Chilterns. It used to be owned by Dirk Bogarde, and was often frequented by Richard Burton and Elizabeth Taylor, but as an irrepressible four-year-old I wasn't much interested in its history; I was far more excited by the two tennis courts in the grounds that were perfect places for Aimee, Kelly and me to drive the child-size, battery-powered cars we were given for Christmas one year. We must have loved those things, because I can remember there being a whole load of them over the years, but the three that really stick in my mind were Aimee's black Corvette, Kelly's Barbie-pink sports car and my white Jeep.

Beel House may have been a rock star's mansion, but it was also a homely kind of place, warm, comforting and safe – a security blanket of a house. We went to the local school – the Gateway School in Great Missenden – like ordinary kids, played with our pets and our toys like ordinary kids, and messed around in the backyard like ordinary kids. I loved that place: there was an amazing tree house in the garden, and fields and forests all around where we would go for walks and see the deer and other animals that grazed on our land. It was idyllic, and I just remember being incredibly happy there, and making good friends. I was Aimee and Kelly's little plaything: they used to find Mum's more outrageous clothes from the 1960s and dress me up in them – make-up, the works. For them, it was a laugh; for me, a self-conscious six-year-old, it was hell! I'm told that one Christmas Eve, when I was much smaller, Aimee came into my bedroom late at night, took me out of my cot, and dragged me downstairs by one arm, like Christopher Robin dragging Winnie-the-Pooh. Mum was only alerted to it when she heard the sound of me bumping down the stairs.

My parents went out of their way to make things fun. It helped, of course, that they were the biggest kids in the world themselves – my dad especially. Birthdays were unforgettable. As we had larger resources than most people, so our birthday celebrations were on an appropriately grandiose scale. It was all pretty extravagant: when birthday time came around, we could pretty much name the party we wanted, and more often than not it would be laid on. And best of all, my parents would get as excited about it as us kids. Mum especially loves to throw a party – she's always up for it, and always does it really well, totally going to town on every last detail. The cakes were particularly impressive – even now she likes to push the boat out, and my last birthday cake was in the shape of a huge mountain with people climbing in it. (A bit different from the cake I had for my seventeenth birthday, which was skilfully fashioned into the shape of a pair of tits. I suppose subtlety has never been our trademark.)

Our birthdays are all pretty close – Kelly's is 27 October, Aimee's is 2 September – so as children we would often have joint parties. Either Aimee and Kelly would share, or Kelly and me. One year, the girls had a circus theme to their party. Most parents would be happy to settle for a clown to entertain the kiddies before the jelly and ice cream. Not mine. To start with, we had an elephant delivered – don't ask me where they got it from, or how it arrived, but it was the centrepiece of an extravaganza that included a whole load of other animals as well as an entire troop of clowns. Pretty exciting stuff for a bunch of toddlers, although I'm told it backfired a little when a few of the guests got frightened of the elephant and ended up screaming for their mummies . . .

The elephant birthday aside, we'd have full-on, carnival-type parties with no expense spared: swings, slides, merry-go-rounds, bouncy castles, plus there would always be a disco afterwards, with the kids hurling themselves around to whatever was big in the world of toddler pop at the time. I seem to remember Chesney Hawkes playing a pretty prominent role. I'm not sure what my dad thought about that, but I'm glad to say my own taste has developed a bit since those teenybopping days.

Dad was away a lot, but he'd always make an effort to be around at birthday time, and when he did there was no way he was going to be a responsible adult standing on the sidelines watching the kids have fun, backslapping with their stockbroker parents and solicitously looking after Little Johnny when he scraped his knee. On the contrary, he'd be the one scraping *his* knee – I remember Mum getting pissed off with him when he used to bound out of nowhere and jump on the bouncy castle, throwing kids all over the place thanks to the fact that my dad was considerably heavier than his playmates.

Christmases, too, were always magical times, largely thanks to the fact that my mum and dad would really pull out the stops to make sure that everything was just right for the kids. The earliest Christmases I can remember were at Beel House, and Dad was always the best fun at Christmas, acting all goofy and generally just fucking around with us kids, playing and really getting into the spirit of things. He would dress up – I don't remember him ever being a particularly convincing Santa Claus, but he used to cover himself in Christmas wrapping paper, which we thought was hilarious as children; and Mum would get just as excited, making enormous Christmas stockings that could easily fit a hyperactive child inside and still leave room for plenty of wriggling, revelling in the fact that her family were all around her, and doing whatever she could to make each Christmas a memorable one for all of us. And of course there is nothing more fun for a young kid than adults joining in. I used to get really obsessed about certain things – one year it would be *Star Wars*, another it would be aliens. This particular Christmas it was the military and I was given a whole bunch of model soldiers and a huge remote control army truck for them all to go in. We were spending Christmas on holiday somewhere hot: it might have been blazing sunshine outside; there might have been golden sands and crystal blue sea; but Dad and I spent three days straight sitting in the hotel room playing with these toy soldiers from breakfast to bedtime.

Even when we weren't stuck inside playing soldiers, childhood holidays were always a lot of fun, even though we seemed to have the same holiday destination year in, year out: Hawaii. My parents have a thing about the place because they got married there in 1982. Their wedding was a bittersweet time for them, if only because Mum's parents didn't seem to give their full support to the whole affair – she had a difficult relationship with them, and I think she was determined that it would never be that way with Kelly, Aimee and me – but still they can't resist the romantic gesture of holidaying in Hawaii as often as they can. It 'holds a special place in their hearts' – so they always tell us. Add to that the fact that Dad is a total creature of habit: we'd be planning the family holiday, and you could write the script before the conversation even started.

Us: 'Where are we going to go this year?'

Dad: 'I don't wanna go anywhere. Let's go to Hawaii. Fuck it.'

I'm sure Dad won't take it the wrong way when I suggest that maybe the fact that it's ideally suited for people who want to sit around drinking and doing fuck all had something to do with it. And so Hawaii it was. Now don't get me wrong, Hawaii is an amazing place, but we went there so often that I've grown to hate it. Most people dream about going there, I know, but visit it forty times and you might find yourself looking at the grass shirts and floral garlands a bit differently – the novelty of this tropical paradise starts to wear off, unless you're my mum and dad. Nowadays I dream about going anywhere but!

As a kid, though, it was a laugh, especially when there was a whole bunch of us out there. Dad would sometimes do a show on the island, and Mum would always try to make sure it was the last show of the tour so that everyone would be able to hang out there for a few days afterwards – forty members of the Ozzy Osbourne entourage in the same hotel at the end of a tour is a pretty reliable recipe for a good time, especially when you're just a kid. And as we got older, we'd be allowed to bring friends along, which was always a blast.

The only other holiday destination that was ever considered was Antigua. Dad had this old manager from the Black Sabbath days called Patrick Meehan who ended up purchasing this condo resort on the island. For a while, Dad really loved it there, and it *was* the coolest place. Even as kids we could just walk out of the condo and hitchhike into town – that was what everybody did, and we were no exception. Everyone helped each other out, and it was extremely cool and relaxed.

One time the staff at the condo didn't get paid, and Dad ended up having to put money in their pockets and pay expenses for the whole resort. He was pretty laid back about it, but I remember one occasion when he was standing in the reception using the only phone in the whole place to make a call to Mum and a disgruntled employee came up to him and started waving a knife in his face, demanding to be paid. 'I'm going to kill you!' he shouted. 'Why haven't you paid me? I'm going to kill everyone here!'

Poor Dad took one look at him, then bent double with laughter. There was no denying that there was real anger in the guy's eyes, but unfortunately the knife he was wielding was only about an inch long and attached to his key ring. He'd have had trouble cutting a loaf of bread with it, let alone a 200-pound rock star. But that was just how it seemed to be in Antigua – even the psychos were harmless.

We went to Hawaii more recently with the MTV

cameras in tow, filming for *The Osbournes*, which made for a slightly different experience and brought home to me how much my life has changed since those early days. Beforehand, even though Dad was well known, at least the rest of the family had a degree of anonymity. Those TV guys aren't exactly ones to be subtle about anything, and of course they had people there in advance sorting everything out and hiring local crew to work for them. So with Hawaii being about the size of a pinhead, local people tell local people, who then tell *everyone* that the Osbournes are arriving. When we got there, we turned on the car radio and instead of reading the weather, the announcer is yelling, 'And today, folks, Hawaii welcomes the Osbournes!' The paparazzi were out in force, helicopters were flying over the hotel – it was all a far cry from the holidays I remembered as a kid. It was nice to have the attention in a way, but kind of hard to relax.

Growing up, though, I was pretty much shielded from that kind of media interest. The paparazzi were never really that interested in the family before we became TV celebrities in our own right. Dad was just a rock musician, and press photographers rarely paid that much attention to him. He was hardly a beautiful young thing, so he didn't end up on the front page of the paper very often. Our family was known among his fans and in the music industry, but on the whole those people were pretty respectful. So celebrity was never really a concept I had to get used to, and I grew up able to enjoy the good bits about my dad's fame, and not be plagued by the shitty bits.

It seems like a whole other life away . . .

*

My dad loves to tell stories. It's the performer in him, I suppose, that makes him such a great raconteur. As a child, I used to love listening to him tell tales about his own childhood, and in doing so he perhaps inadvertently taught me a lot about my own background.

Growing up in post-war Birmingham was a far cry from growing up in the peaceful corner of the Chilterns where my formative years were spent, but there were nevertheless some strange parallels between my father's teenage life and mine. I never knew my paternal grandparents – my grandfather died before I was born, and although my grandmother lived until I was about fifteen, I never met her. I think Dad had something of a love–hate relationship with his parents, and it's hardly surprising: the industrial Midlands in the late 1940s and early 50s wasn't the happiest of places, and that household was no exception to the general hardship and poverty. Dad says that the film *Angela's Ashes* pretty much brings it all back to him. Even now I don't think he's forgotten what it was like, and as a result he has never become arrogant about his fame. The way he will walk into a room and, despite the fact that he is well known, will do his best to blend into the background is one of his most endearing qualities, and reflects greatly on how he was as a child. His dad worked night shifts at a local factory; his mum did factory work too, and the impression I get from him is that he harboured a lot of resentment against his mum because she didn't really care for him as much as he would have liked. He has two brothers and three sisters, so it was a big family for people of such small means – no new clothes, one bath a week and eight of them cramped into a tiny house with only two bedrooms – but I think Dad could have coped with all that if there had just been a little bit more love and care to go around.

As it was, it was an abusive household: you step out of line, you get fucked up. My grandfather was a heavy drinker. I guess everyone was at the time – it was all they really had, the only way they could escape from the drudgery of their day-to-day existence – and when the alcohol-induced red mist descended, he wouldn't think twice about raising a hand to his children. But if he thought that kind of discipline would keep his son in line, he was wrong. My dad was an absolute terror as a kid, by all accounts, and he relishes telling hilarious tales of his antics as a young boy.

My grandfather would come home from work absolutely shattered. Occasionally, he would have a few drinks and then fall asleep fully clothed on the bed. One day, Dad managed to get hold of a big staple gun. He tiptoed up to my grandfather's bed as he lay sleeping, then stapled all his clothes – with him still in them – to the mattress. He hid the staple gun, then came running into the room screaming at the top of his voice. 'Fire! There's a fire! There's a fire!'

My grandfather woke with a start and tried to jump up; but his son had done a very good job of stapling him to the bed, and he couldn't move a muscle. When Dad used to tell us this story as kids, we would shriek with laughter. 'What happened next, Dad?'

'I got the shit kicked out of me.'

It seemed that lots of his childhood stories ended that way.

Some men get aggressive when they start drinking. With my grandfather it was the other way round. He would come home from work, get totally stressed out with my grandmother, and more often than not he

would start slapping her around. Then he'd storm out of
the house to the working-men's drinking spot where he
spent nearly all of his time, occasionally calling at my
dad to follow him. Dad would spend hours on end
sitting outside, waiting for my grandfather to drink his
fill and then marvelling at the fact that he had turned
from this aggressive wife-beater into something far more
jolly. And all thanks to beer – it was like some kind of
magic potion. He was only fourteen when one of the
men in the pub took pity on him having to wait around
outside all the time and gave him his first ever pint of
beer. He drank six pints that night, got totally drunk and
passed out. It was the beginning of an addiction that
would plague him all his life, but in a way he never stood
a chance. Everyone drank: there was nothing else to do.

Despite his aggressiveness, I think my dad respected
his father. But no amount of respect, and no amount of
beatings, were going to stop him getting into trouble.
During the war, all the towns around had been blown up
and practically razed to the ground; as a kid, he would
always go and play in the bombed-out building sites. It's
a miracle he and his friends weren't killed in those
places. One day, Dad was on the first floor of some
building, jumping up and down on a mattress, when the
floor gave way. He fell through the ceiling to find himself in a Home Guard armoury, stashed full of guns and
ammunition – a treasure trove for a bored kid. Dad
picked out a hand grenade and nonchalantly took it to
the local museum. 'How much will you give me for this?'
he asked the curator.

The museum staff, of course, were less than
impressed that some urchin had walked on to the
premises with a live hand grenade. The police were
called out, and then the bomb squad. From his stories,

it's clear that the young Ozzy was hell-raising from an early age.

He was the archetypal problem child: always getting the shit kicked out of him at home because he was doing something stupid. He wanted a bike, but his parents couldn't afford one, so he went down to the scrapyard and nicked a bike frame and some wheels. But he could never find a seat, so he just had this bike with a pole, and obviously he could never sit down when he was riding it. One day, however, the pedals fell off his hotch-potch contraption: he landed on the pole and I'm sure I don't need to describe the consequences in too much detail. Painful for my dad; hilarious to hear about when you're seven years old.

For Dad, school was a nightmare. It was a five mile walk to Birchfield Road Secondary Modern, and he hated every step he had to take. He suffered from all kinds of learning difficulties, but of course this was in the days before people had learned to diagnose and treat such things, so he just got slapped about by his teachers, and sent home for being stupid or for not doing his homework. With a couple of friends he started playing truant more and more regularly, relieved not to have to be subjected to the torment of school life, and they would just fuck around – nicking sweets, scrumping apples, all the usual kinds of stuff tearaway kids in poor areas did. And it was hardly surprising that he left school as soon as he possibly could, working in a series of dead-end jobs, before ending up in a slaughterhouse.

He would love telling us his slaughterhouse stories. He worked in this slaughterhouse for ages, the world's most miserable job – killing animals all day long. You name it, he killed it: cows, pigs, chickens, lambs. His first job there was to cut up 6,000 sheep's stomachs. The place was overrun with rats, and he used to tell us a gory story about one guy who cut his finger on a knife then touched some rat piss. He died a week later. Another time he had a date with a girl. He turned up and gave her a present: she unwrapped it to find a cow's eye. 'Something to see you through the week,' my dad told her. Suffice to say that the relationship was a non-starter. The only way he could deal with the horrors of the slaughterhouse was through alcohol – he got blind drunk every day in an attempt to forget about it.

And then there were the days on the road with Black Sabbath: taking acid on a beach, then diving off some beach tower into the sand, thinking it was water. Playing three shows a day in some random club in Sweden and being paid so little that they never had enough to eat. They'd meet girls, go home with them, rob their refrigerators and then just leg it!

But despite the funny stories, my dad had a difficult upbringing, and he started battling demons that kids shouldn't have to deal with. He retreated into himself, and became lost in a sea of depression that threatened to engulf him. One night he went outside and took his mum's clothesline down. He turned it into a noose, which he put round his neck, tied one end to something solid and high up, then jumped off a chair. Luckily for him, his dad came home at exactly that moment and got him down.

Dad's only escape from that world was his music, but it didn't make him any closer to his family. They were traditional members of the British working class, and suddenly he was a rock star with all the trappings that the lifestyle entailed. He left the Birmingham of his childhood behind, and lost the ability to relate to his parents in any way. In recent years he's become closer to his siblings – his sisters more so than his brothers – and his nephew Terry, who we call Cousin Terry, has become close to our family. He's appeared in *The X Factor* and *The Salon*, so is more on Dad's wavelength; but Dad himself has left that abusive, working-class Midlands family life far behind.

Mum, too, had a rocky relationship with her parents. Her father is Don Arden, a well-known, if slightly shady, music promoter. Mum worked for him from the time she was old enough to do so, and he completely took advantage of her during that time. He also represented my dad – which is how they met, their relationship being sealed when she took over Dad's management and ensured he had a successful solo career once he left Sabbath. My grandfather is very sick now, his mind shot with Alzheimer's disease, but for all the time I was growing up I thought he was dead – because that's what Mum told me. They fell out in such a big way, and he treated her so badly, bullying her, demeaning her, sapping her self-respect, that she didn't want us to have any contact with him.

It wasn't until I was a teenager that she came clean and told us that we had a grandfather after all. I was pretty pissed off at the time that she had lied to us for so long. I'd have preferred to know the truth, that he was just a horrible man, but I guess she had her reasons – he was, after all, very shitty towards her. When I finally met him, it was before he started to become very ill, before it was clear that he was approaching the end of his life. He seemed to me to be an OK kind of guy, but I could see that he was making a real effort, and that actually he had a mean streak in him. My grandfather seemed to me to be like a fast-talking cross between a New York gangster and a shady second-hand car dealer. He made an effort to be nice to me, and we hung out a few times, though we never had any heart-to-hearts, never really got to know each other.

Then the illness started to get a hold on him. It's a strange condition, Alzheimer's disease. There would be some days when my mum, or some nurse he'd had for ages, would walk in and he would be able to recount a conversation they'd had years ago; but there would also be times when my mum would go and see him and it would be another story. 'Who the hell are you? Am I supposed to know you? I've no idea who you are.' I haven't seen him for a few years now, but I know Mum finds it really tough and has a lot of mixed feelings about her responsibilities to him.

So, having had upbringings that were starved of affection, my parents went out of their way to ensure that history did not repeat itself. It was difficult, though. Dad was on the road, and Mum was managing him, so they were often both away from home for extended periods of time. Mum would always make sure that she was never away from home for more than two weeks at a time, three weeks tops – she would fly back from wherever she was to be with us – but even when she was at home, because so much of Dad's work was in America and the Far East, she would be up all night on the phone, then working during the day as well. We didn't have the nine-to-five consistency of most families, so the only way the household could possibly work was with the help of nannies.

That's not to say that we had an absent mother. Far from it. Mum was completely involved in our lives and did everything she could to make home as homely as it could be. If she was away, she would write each of us a little letter to open every day of her absence, telling us how much she missed us and was thinking of us, and she would call before school and after school, checking up on us and saying she loved us. And when she was at home, we saw her every day, and she took an interest in absolutely everything we did. She always claims she can't cook, but that's not true: every Sunday there would be Sunday lunch on the table, cooked by her. As a result, I grew into a full-on mummy's boy, and still am to this day. She was never that strict about me going to school, and I loved spending the day with her while she went about her business. So more than once, I'd say to her, 'Mum, do I have to go to school?'

'Do you want to go to school?'

'Not really.'

'Then don't.'

So I didn't. Instead I'd spend my time hanging out with Mum, going shopping, going to hair appointments, going to work meetings and watching her do what she did so well.

But I couldn't spend every day with her. She was a full-time working mother, so nannies were our only option. They would wake us up, take us to school, pick us up again, cook most of our meals – just because our parents had to work.

And boy did we get through a ton of nannies.

I couldn't even begin to count them, but it must have been at least thirty.

One thing I've learned is how hard it is to find a good nanny, someone with whom you feel confident leaving your kids for extended periods of time. In a way, they need to have some of the qualities of the parents, because there's no way you want to leave your children with somebody who is completely different from you in every way. But although nobody could say my folks are exactly conventional, they looked positively strait-laced compared to some of the psychos that ended up being entrusted with our care. Obviously we had some great nannies but the bad ones were truly bad.

There would always be some weird shit going on with some of them. One of them was really verbally abusive and would let rip at us at the slightest provocation; another had this obsession with dirty vegetables and would insist on eating them raw and covered in muck. There were nannies who would get drunk and start flirting with Dad right in front of Mum – they'd be gone the very next day – and nannies who were more untidy than us kids, who refused to clean anything up and basically do their job. I even got set on fire by a nanny once. I was a little kid at the time, still in nappies, but I remember it clearly. At her interview she lied to Mum and said she didn't smoke, but she did. A few days later she was driving me somewhere, cigarette in hand. I was in the back seat with my window open slightly, so when she threw the cigarette butt out of her window, it flew straight into mine and landed on me. It's amazing how combustible kids can be. I don't remember many more details about that nanny, like whether she was nice or nasty, but I do remember being pretty upset that I'd been set on fire.

As a little boy I was always terribly afraid of carwashes. Don't ask me why, I just felt like I was going into the mouth of a demon. It wasn't just a vague sense of unease; I was truly and genuinely petrified and would scream my little lungs out if I had to go into one. It didn't matter to this one nanny we had, who insisted on taking me through the car-wash every afternoon after school. She must have been a fucking lunatic – either that or she thought it was part of her remit to treat me with aversion therapy, because it never seemed to occur

to her that she could have the car washed when I wasn't
there.

One October, Kelly and I had a joint Halloween
party as it fell right in the middle of our two birthdays.
It was a big event, and a lot of family friends were
invited. And where there were adults, there was alcohol
and lots of it. Our nanny at the time got a little bit the
worse for wear. Actually, that's something of an under-
statement. She got absolutely obliterated and vomited all
over the place.

Unfortunately, Dad followed suit. He got helplessly
drunk, stripped down to his underwear and stood in the
hallway to our house singing cheesy pop songs at the top
of his voice, with the nanny violently puking in the background. It was at that exact moment that my friend
Robert had to leave. His parents were very proper
people – Robert is now training to be an army officer at
Sandhurst – and the first sight they were greeted with
was a drunk, almost naked Ozzy in full song dancing in
the hallway, and a copiously vomiting nanny. The look
on their faces was a picture.

So nannies came and went. But I don't want to give
the impression that we were a bunch of spoiled little
brats, playing them up and making their lives hell. It's
not like we were good as gold all the time, but we were
just ordinary kids, doing what ordinary kids do. Somehow, though, we just seemed to attract the weirdos. I
was always perfectly nice to them, no matter what their
idiosyncrasies. In fact, as a kid, that was me through
and through: I was always polite, nice and loving. It's a
quality that I don't really like in myself that much, this
need to please people, to get on with anyone – I just find
it easier to bite the bullet and stay friends with everyone.
Aimee and Kelly would clash with them all the time, but

it would take a lot for me to dislike a nanny to the point that we would all be complaining about her to Mum. But it did sometimes happen that we would have to close ranks, go to her and say, 'Look, Mum, we need to get rid of this woman. She's a lunatic.' And when that happened, she'd be gone. Mum trusted our opinion in the matter implicitly, and she knew that if it got to the point where the three of us unanimously decided we were unhappy with a nanny, she would get rid of them without a second thought. We responded well to the trust that was put in us, only taking things to Mum if our personalities and the nanny's were genuinely at loggerheads. And there *were* good nannies, people who we are still in touch with now. There was a woman called Kim, for example, who was absolutely fantastic. She came from Newcastle and Aimee, Kelly and I were page boy and bridesmaids at her wedding.

Unfortunately, though, it was always the good nannies that would leave; the psychos always wanted to stay on. What it was about the family that attracted them, I don't know, but it was definitely true that beneath the fun and the mayhem, there was a darker side to our life that refused to go away . . .

TWO

A FAMILY AFFAIR

Ever since I was old enough to understand it, I've known that my dad was an alcoholic and a drug addict. Truth to tell, I never realised that his addictions weren't normal; I just thought that it was what dads did. And I never really remember getting that upset by it, even though it sent my mum and sisters into floods of tears. For me, it was different. I was pretty much raised by women – my mum, nannies, older sisters – and as Dad was away such a lot because of his career, I missed him. I missed having that male stimulation, and the fact that he was a lot of fun when he was around, and we got on so well, made me even more aware of his absence when he was gone. There were times, though, even when he was not on the road, that he wasn't the most present of father figures, because he was out getting drunk or getting high.

Like most little boys, I looked up to my dad. I wanted to be like him, to mimic him in all kinds of ways. And I remember occasionally seeing him taking a load of pills, or maybe getting drunk and a little crazy, and rather than being scared of him, scared of the stuff he would do, I used to have little childhood fantasies about wanting to do the same thing. It might sound weird, but actually I think it was kind of normal. If your dad's a policeman, you want to dress like a policeman; if your dad's a fireman, you want to get a fireman's hat. I'd see my dad taking pills, and I would go to the shop and buy myself a box of Tic-Tacs. Then I would bring them home and swallow them down – just to be like him. At no point did I feel anything approaching anger towards him; I was never cross about the way he acted when he was under the influence of whatever substance he was abusing at the time; I never thought, You bastard, what are you doing? Why would I? He was my dad, and I loved him.

It's funny how, when you're young, the strangest things can shape your opinion of what's good and what's bad. If there was an exception to my somewhat blasé attitude towards Dad's substance abuse, it was formed of all things by watching the movie *Robocop* on TV. I remember seeing characters in that film snorting cocaine, and it being spoken about as if it were the devil itself, the worst thing someone could possibly do. And that white powder, the stuff they were putting up their noses on TV, was the same stuff that I knew my dad meddled with. Something clicked in my brain: *that's* what it is, I thought to myself. And from that day on, I had this total, almost obsessive, hatred for the stuff. Even when I started going down the path of drug abuse myself, I never touched cocaine. Not once. It was just something that seemed to have been drilled into me from an early age. But the other stuff didn't really worry me: the beers, the spirits, the bottles of pills – I didn't know what they contained, but I knew Dad liked them.

Nothing fazed me. Even when Mum would take me to one side and try to explain Dad's behaviour to me, it was just something I took in my stride. 'Dad's sick,' she would tell me when he had to go into rehab. 'He has to go away because he likes drinking too much.' But I had always just known that it was part and parcel of who my dad was: a musician, a rock star, and this was all just part of the lifestyle. My sisters would get really upset about it and start crying, and I do remember thinking, Well, I guess I *should* be kind of upset about all this. But I wasn't. It wasn't that I was incredibly happy with the situation, but I refused to feel forced sadness.

It became normality. Sometimes dad was drunk and he was funny; sometimes he was drunk and things weren't good. I remember once when we were supposed to go as a family to some friends' house. Dad was drunk and started getting really angry for some reason – maybe he didn't want to go. He picked up a vase and smashed it down on the floor. As he did so, Mum packed us all into the car and drove off, leaving Dad to his fury and his drunkenness. I must have been young at the time, because on that occasion I didn't really understand what was happening, and I kept asking my mum why Dad wasn't coming with us.

I don't know what she replied, but I do know that the best was done to protect us from the worst of Dad's antics. We got home from school one day and some friends of my parents were there at the door, waiting for us to return. 'Let's go for a walk,' they suggested.

'Why can't we go home?' I asked.

'Not now, Jack,' I was told. 'It's not a good time.'

With the insight a child so often has, I could tell when things were getting bad between Mum and Dad. The tension would gradually build up over days and weeks, and then it would explode in a flurry of matrimonial violence – on my mum's part as well as my dad's. When I was small, I would stay out of the way; but as I grew up, it became more difficult to ignore, and on occasion I became involved. Mum threw away some of Dad's pills once. He was furious and started pushing her around. I didn't like seeing my mum treated in this way, so I pushed Dad to his knees, then ran away before I could face up to the consequences of his anger.

Mum wasn't blameless. Although her reasons for wanting Dad to stay away from drink and drugs were for the best, she occasionally dealt with his addiction in ways that were bound to wind him up. We were in Hawaii once, at the end of a tour. My room (which I was sharing with my friend Kevin, son of Bobby, who had worked for my parents for years) was connected to Mum and Dad's room. One day, Dad was sitting out on his balcony smoking pot. He overdid it, and got really fucked up. Mum was so pissed off with him that she found his bag of pot, removed the contents and then shat inside it. Needless to say, when Dad tried to roll his next joint he went absolutely nuts. He ranted and raved in his room, but was too far gone to do anything about it, so he passed out on the bed.

Once he was asleep, Mum and Kelly went into the room and started squirting him with water to wake him up. When he did so, he was furious. I was asleep in the next room, and I heard this shouting and the sound of Dad banging on the door between our two rooms. Kevin and I ran out; when we returned a while later, we saw that Dad had been hitting the door so hard that it had become dislodged from its frame and had to be replaced.

In the back of my mind, I was aware that other people knew about my dad's drug and alcohol addictions. It wasn't that they talked to me directly about it, but I think my peer group knew about my dad as a result of their parents talking about him. They were obviously told never to mention it to me, that it was a sensitive subject, and by and large they respected that. Oh, there were the occasional comments, snide remarks about what a crazy motherfucker Ozzy Osbourne was, but in general Dad's drinking and using were off-limits subjects for my friends.

There are some things you can't ignore, though. I was only very small when my dad tried to kill my mum under the influence of fuck knows what. We didn't see it happening because we were in bed at the time; it was only much later in life that we found out what happened that night. The two of them had been having terrible fights for a while. It's something that has happened throughout their marriage. They love each other more than life itself, but somehow they always used to end up at each other's throats – literally on this occasion. Dad had been drinking really heavily for a few days, downing bottles of vodka and the like, and then one night he came down and started acting all weird with Mum. 'We've decided that you have to die,' he told her.

The first thing Mum did, thank God, was hit the panic button that was connected straight to the local police station. While she was desperately waiting for the cops to arrive, Dad grappled her to the ground with his hands round her throat and tried to strangle her. She managed to get away and lock herself in the bathroom until help came.

The first I knew of it was that there were police cars all around, their blue lights flashing out the front. I was sitting on the upstairs landing with Aimee and Kelly, looking down at the scene through the banisters and seeing my dad, wearing nothing but his underpants, being handcuffed and carted away. My sisters were crying, and so was my mum, and I can remember being upset that they were sad, but otherwise just a bit confused by the whole weird situation. And the next thing I knew we were back in our bedrooms, with someone sitting with us for comfort, until we fell asleep.

And the next day, Dad wasn't there.

It was all over the papers, of course, and that was one of those times that my peer group couldn't help but ask me about it. That afternoon, my mum picked me up from school. 'Did you have a good day?' she asked me.

'Yeah, it was fine,' I shrugged.

'Did anyone mention anything to you?'

'About what?'

'About your dad.'

'Yes,' I told Mum, perfectly honestly.

'What did they say, Jack?'

'They say my dad kills people.'

God knows how that must have made my mum feel. 'You know that's not true, don't you, Jack?' she said.

'Yeah,' I replied.

'How do you know?'

'Well,' I told her in earnest. 'I counted up everyone I know, and nobody's missing, so he can't have killed anyone.'

Dad was hauled up in front of a court, but my mum refused to press charges. Instead he was ordered to go into rehab – not for the first time, and not for the last – and a few weeks later he was back home.

A family man once more.

It always seems strange to me that people can grow up in the same house, with the same parents, all essentially learning the same things and being brought up in the same way, and still be so totally different to each other.

That's the way it is with me and my sisters: we're a close-knit family, but so different in so many ways.

I don't see a whole lot of Aimee. It's a weird kind of relationship where we don't really talk all that much; and although that's changed a bit recently, there have been times when we haven't spoken for seven or eight months. Kelly and I were always very close as kids, but I remember Aimee always being very much The Older Sister, always kind of bossy, always arguing with the nannies and being generally lippy. When she was eight years old she decided she wanted to go to boarding school. We all thought it was the stupidest thing ever – why would you want to go and live by somebody else's rules? – but that's what she wanted to do, and that's what she did. Kelly and I used to hang out together a lot, but Aimee always seemed a bit more closed off. In fact, I never really remember seeing her being particularly happy as a child. She had a lot of trouble with depression as a teenager, and it's still something I think she battles against. The bottom line is that she's an extremely sensitive woman, but sometimes it comes out the wrong way.

If you were to meet her, though, you'd never get an impression of that slightly stroppy side of her character. She's very quiet, very polite. It's not like she will just sit there and ignore you, but she just doesn't tend to draw attention to herself. But I've never seen a person's personality shift so much when she gets a few drinks inside her: she becomes much more of a party girl.

Kelly and I are much closer, and our lives are much more intertwined – we work together, and she still lives with Mum and Dad in LA, so whenever I go to the house, she's there. She's a funny old character. As a little girl she would cry all the time, every morning. She had this really long, platinum hair that went right down to the middle of her back, and each morning she'd come down to have it brushed by Mum or the nanny, and she would just sit there and scream her heart out. If she didn't like something, she'd cry. If she didn't like some-*one*, she'd cry.

Of course, sometimes she had more reason to cry than others. When I was a child, Dad and I used to have a joint obsession with firearms, and I even had my own air rifle. Dad and I used to practise shooting these rifles from the kitchen door, firing at targets hung on a nearby barn. Boys will be boys, and it was a pretty cool way to pass the time – we even used to dress up in army fatigues to do it. One day, he and Mum had gone to New York so that Dad could film a part in a movie. They were gone for ten or twelve days, so we were being baby-sat by his guitarist, Zakk Wylde, and his wife Barbaranne. Little Jack decided he wanted to do some shooting, so I snuck away and took up my position in our usual place at the kitchen door. There were dogs running around all over the place, with Kelly chasing after them.

'Hey, Kelly,' I called to my sister. 'Get the dogs out of the way.'

And that's exactly what I thought she would do. I certainly didn't imagine that she would run in front of me. I lined up my telescopic sights with the target, and just as I squeezed the trigger I saw her leg appear in front of my eyes. You know those moments in your life when you can feel everything happening in slow-mo? Well, this was one of them. The instant I felt the gun fire, I saw everything like an action replay on TV. 'Please,' I whispered to myself, 'No! Don't let this be happening!' My stomach lurched – the reflex action of a kid who knows he's just done something that's going to get him into a *load* of trouble.

It was a .22 gauge air rifle – a pretty big bullet – and it went right through Kelly's calf muscle and out the other side.

I remember that day like it was yesterday: the beautiful sunshine; the T-shirt and shorts Kelly and I were both wearing; my sister screaming and crying because I'd just shot a bullet through her leg. Zakk and Barbaranne took her to the hospital, where they glued up the wound and gave her some antibiotics. They told her it was only a tiny hole, but it didn't seem to mollify Kelly – she hasn't let me forget that little incident ever since. And I suppose she's got a right to be kind of pissed that her little brother shot her.

I think my parents came to the same conclusion: it was a while before I was allowed to don khaki and go hunting with my dad again – for rabbits, this time, not sisters. Back then the fields surrounding the house were overrun with the little things, and Dad taught me how to shoot them and skin them. We never ate our catch though, as they were riddled with myxomatosis. Come to think of it, that was probably the only reason we managed to shoot them in the first place.

As anyone who has seen her on TV will know, Kelly is a real handful: incredibly opinionated, incredibly feisty. And she enjoys a good drama, as a story that has gone down in the annals of Osbourne history shows. When we were living at Beel House, our bedrooms were separated by a hallway at the top of the stairs, with a walkway leading off it from which you could see the front door. Kelly walked out there one day, and suddenly started screaming her head off. As quick as a flash, Mum, Dad and Tony (Dad's personal assistant, who we call Uncle Tony because he's been around for as long as we can remember) come sprinting up the stairs. 'What's wrong, Kelly? What's wrong?'

Still screaming, Kelly pointed towards the front door. 'There's a robber! I just saw a robber outside!'

Everyone totally freaks out and starts running around like headless chickens. The police are called out in a matter of seconds, then Tony takes Kelly to one side, sits her down and starts talking to her. 'OK, Kelly,' he tries to calm my hysterical sister. 'You need to think carefully. Do you remember what this guy looked like?'

Kelly nods her head. 'Yes.'

'Can you describe him?'

'Yes.'

'Go on then.'

'OK. He had a black and white striped shirt on, and a mask over his eyes.'

'I see,' says Tony. 'Tell me, Kelly, did he have a bag over his shoulder that said "Swag"?'

'Yes,' Kelly tells him, eyes wide with honesty. And that was the end of that little crisis . . .

To this day, Kelly will exaggerate. I might walk into her room and say, 'Hi, Kell!' But it will get translated to her friends very differently: 'Fucking Jack, he barges into the room, called me a motherfucker and all this shit, then storms out. I'll fucking get him . . .' She perceives things the way she wants to: it can be kind of endearing at times, and at other times it can just be fucking annoying. But at the end of the day, Kelly is a genuinely sweet, affectionate person who has a lot of love for a lot of people, and no matter if our lives start taking us in different directions, we'll always be incredibly close – just so long as I can keep from shooting her again.

*

Mum's work took her away from home a lot, normally
to America, and she started finding it increasingly difficult being away from us. It ripped her apart every time
she had to say goodbye to her babies. So, when I was six
years old, the decision was made for the whole family to
up sticks and move to Los Angeles. The area my parents
chose was Pacific Palisades – a far cry from the leafy
countryside of Buckinghamshire. Close to the beaches
of Malibu, Santa Monica Bay and the Santa Monica
mountains, it's an incredibly well-to-do area that's perfect for families: safe, with wide open spaces and good
schools. At the time, the area had yet to become popular
with celebrities, and despite the fact that it was a very
well-heeled, predominantly Christian neighbourhood,
the Osbourne family were welcomed there with open
arms. That's the way LA is – if you're famous, they kiss
your ass, as I was to find out later in my life.

We lived in a part of the Palisades called the
Highlands, which overlooks the ocean, and my parents
enrolled me at a Christian school, which was an absolutely fantastic place. It was a nice, family-run school on
an amazing campus really close to home. My parents
loved it, and it was a safe, secure environment for me. It
looked like you would imagine an Ivy League university
would look like. And although it was a Christian school,
there was nothing too evangelical about it – we'd have
to pray, and there were Bible classes every week, but
apart from that it was just a normal place full of normal,
well-adjusted children. I liked my teacher and we
learned all the regular things that children learn at
school. There was a maths test every week, and a
spelling test, and all our reading material was prescribed
for us; but I didn't find it easy to keep up with the
others academically. The spelling always seemed to elude

me, and keeping my concentration up was always a problem for me. As a result, even at that age I was always the joker, the funny-guy in the class

I didn't get much of a chance to settle in there, though, because a year later we moved back to the UK. Mum had fallen in love with another house, not too far from Beel House and similarly luxurious. Welders House is tucked away off a tiny country road that is itself like something out of a picture book. If you didn't know it was there, you'd probably drive right past it. But behind the security gates and the cameras is a striking Victorian house, all oak panels and chandeliers, surrounded by fields and woods – another perfect place to grow up. The house itself was built by Disraeli for his daughter as a wedding present, but soon enough Mum had made her mark on it. The whole of the top floor was given over to us children, and she had the ceiling painted blue with white clouds to resemble the sky. We went back to the same schools we had left a year or so before, and hung out with the same friends – it was almost as if nothing had changed. Mum and Dad would take us out into the woods, where we would play all day long in the summer; sometimes we would take the quad bikes to farthest corners of the grounds just to explore; other times we'd take our bicycles out into the hills with a picnic and stay out playing till evening.

It wasn't to be the last time that my family crossed the Atlantic – for the next few years we switched countries almost as often as most people switched cars. Strangely, I didn't find it too disruptive. Even when we moved back to America again when I was a bit older, I stayed in touch with friends in England, and some of them remain close friends to this day. I guess I was lucky: I've spoken to countless people who grew up in between countries, or whose parents joined the military and so took them all over the world, and they found it very difficult to put down roots and keep friends. Somehow I never seemed to have that problem.

And if I'm honest, I had another reason for not minding switching between countries. It may not have disrupted my home and social life, but it couldn't help but affect my school life; and to be frank, I liked it that way. I had come to hate school. There always seemed to be a million and one other things I would rather be doing and, like my dad before me, I always seemed to be getting into trouble. But just when things were coming to a head, just when it became clear that there was going to be a major clampdown on young Jack Osbourne's behaviour, we would make another move across the Atlantic, and suddenly the problem would go away.

It didn't help, of course, that I was told I had dyslexia at the age of eight – one in a line of learning difficulties that I was to be diagnosed with over the next few years. Dyslexia is a reading difficulty that is not due to any obvious causes, such as bad eyesight or bad hearing. I don't remember it bothering me much – I might have had difficulties concentrating on my schoolwork, but for me the dyslexia was just another reason not to want to go to school. And Mum and Dad were never that strict about my attendance. They couldn't be. After all, they both left school at the earliest opportunity, and were never exactly the world's foremost academics. Add to that the fact that they felt bad that they were always jetting off, and it became easy for me to persuade them to let me stay away from school. Mum especially. She was always kind of clingy with us, and just liked having her children around her, so she would often get as excited as we were about us staying off school.

From a really early age I was used to spending summers with Dad and the rest of the family on tour; but when I was ten or eleven I just didn't fucking bother going to school for a couple of months, and spent the whole winter on the road too. It was a much cooler way to spend my time than being in class. We were touring Europe and, my dad being who he was, I became really friendly with the production team and the roadies. I even started helping out. Imagine it – doing roadie work at the age of ten. I would be out there every night, striking the stage and pretty much doing full-on manual labour – coiling ropes and all that kind of physical shit.

Life on the road was never that big a deal for me. None of that stuff was. One of my earliest memories is of being at a video shoot for the hard rock band The Quireboys, who Mum was managing at the time, and it was all impressive and over-the-top, as these things normally are. But at the time I was totally unfazed by it, by how grand it was and the incredible scale of the thing. I guess I was just born in to it, and had been used to it for as long as I could remember, simply seeing it as being my dad's job. Going on tour was like going to work with my dad, the same as lots of my friends occasionally did.

But at the same time it was never boring: hanging out as part of a huge rock tour was always going to be exciting for three little kids. Aimee, Kelly and I would just run riot all over the place, entranced by all the cool stuff there was around: walkie-talkies, monitors, microphones, catering. We were more spoiled on the road than we were at home, because we could just ask for something and there would be someone there to get it for us. One day I said to one of the production staff, 'Hey, I want a PlayStation.' Sure enough, an hour later a PlayStation appears. It was like that with anything we asked for.

And of course, we were the typical boss's kids, being completely mischievous and seeing just what we could get away with. I never played the 'I'm the boss's son' card, and if I'm honest I would have to say that our mischief was never guilt-free; but at the back of our mind we were aware that everybody *knew* who we were, and that meant that we could push the envelope a little. On one occasion I was nabbed by security for fooling around, and taken to a kind of in situ police station that the venue had. I didn't say anything to the security guy about who I was – it wasn't until we walked past one of the tour security guys that all hell broke loose. But despite the risk and the paranoia of getting caught – or maybe because of it – it was such fun, terrorising these shows and the venues we were at, causing havoc at every available opportunity and feeding off each other. Sometimes, if we really pushed things too far, we'd get in trouble and be hauled up in front of Mum to be yelled at – there's nothing worse as a kid than being told off in front of everyone, feeling the hot flush of embarrassment rising up your neck, with all eyes on you. But more often than not, Mum would cut us some slack and, when she heard of our latest misdemeanour, just laugh it off and leave us to our own devices once more. And of course, when it came to reprimanding us, it didn't help that on occasion it was the grown-ups who were pranking around more than us: I remember Dad persuading some of the stage crew to throw flour and eggs at one of the bands on stage once. Kelly, Aimee and I just sat in the wings laughing hysterically like it was the funniest thing we'd ever seen.

Sometimes, though, the excitement veered over to the wrong side of what was appropriate for small children on the road. On one occasion, Dad was playing a tribute concert to Randy Rhoads, a guitar player of his who had died ten years previously. He had been on the road with Mum and Dad when he took a trip in a small airplane. The plane got out of control and crashed – its wing actually clipped the tour bus in which Dad was resting – and then just turned into a blazing fireball. Dad was really lucky not to be injured, but both he and Mum were absolutely devastated at the loss of Randy: he was one of the best rock guitarists in the world, but he was also an incredibly close friend. So Dad was happy to perform at this massive show in his home town. It was held at this absolutely colossal outdoor venue – they call these places 'sheds' in America – with maybe 12,000 seats covered by a huge canopy roof, and a grass lawn behind them with enough room for another fifteen or twenty thousand people. During the concert I was backstage in the dressing room, and I had fallen asleep. Suddenly I woke up and became aware that there were people in the dressing room that I didn't know, all running amok and stealing shit from right under my nose.

It transpired that what had happened was that Dad, in the full throes of his performance, had shouted out, 'Hey, why doesn't everyone come on down.' He didn't mean it literally, but that's how they had all taken it, and suddenly – whoosh! – everyone was flooding on to the stage. It was really low, so it was easy to get on to, and suddenly there's a full-on riot. People are trying to steal guitars out of the guitar rack, even the mike out of Dad's hand, and suddenly he and all the crew guys are having to beat the shit out of people just to defend themselves. You can imagine the scene: thousands of long-haired hard-rock fans, no doubt out of their heads on drugs and alcohol, whipping themselves up into this incredible frenzy and acting with a crazy mob mentality. It seemed kind of exciting at the time, but looking back I suppose it was actually pretty scary, especially for the people looking after us kids. When the crowd got backstage and into the dressing rooms, I was quickly grabbed and thrown in a van to be driven away to safety; but I remember looking back at all the pandemonium kicking off and seeing Dad having a full-blown fist fight on the stage.

There was always some sort of drama on Dad's tours, some sort of excitement, and it wasn't always good. A fan fell off a balcony one time and busted his head open. He ended up in a coma and Dad had to go to the hospital to see him. On another occasion, when my dad failed to turn up at one of the Ozzfest festival tours that Mum started organising in the mid-90s, there was another out-and-out riot. Ozzfest was always a massive event, with loads of different bands touring all over north America. This particular gig was in Washington, and was at this huge entertainment facility where, in the foyer, they had a show car on display – like you see at airports sometimes. I can't remember what kind of car it was – a Bentley, perhaps – but when the riot kicked off, a bunch of guys actually stole the fucking car! It was crazy. The fans rushed the stage and they ended up having to get the riot teams out, firing gas canisters into the crowds. I know Dad felt really bad about that one, because despite what people think, beneath it all he's actually a very peaceful, humble man.

It was in the early 90s that Mum first had the idea to start Ozzfest. It was at a time when there were lots of festivals happening, full of a huge cross-section of music catering for all kinds of tastes. One of those festivals was called Lollapalooza, and it was really eclectic – over the years they've had artists as diverse as Sinead O'Connor and the Butthole Surfers. Mum decided that she wanted Dad to be performing at it, so she made the call, only to be told that the promoters didn't think there was an audience for his kind of music. 'He's not relevant,' they said. 'No one wants to go and see Ozzy Osbourne shows any more.'

Mum's really not the kind of person to take no for an answer. She's had it really tough, trying to make it in the male-dominated industry of music management; she's had to fight twice as hard as anyone else to get what she wants. She got so annoyed by the attitude of these festival promoters that she thought, Fuck it, we'll do it ourselves. We'll do our own tour, with our own harder-edged, working-class kind of bands, and we'll prove them wrong.

And so Ozzfest was born. At the first tour in 1996, there were only two shows, in Phoenix and Los Angeles. They sold out immediately. The next year was bigger – twenty-two dates all over America – and still a huge success, and it's been growing in size every year since then. Now it's like a travelling carnival: sixty crew, twenty bands and two stages. The main stage is for the headline acts, the second stage is for the up-and-coming ones. It has become *the* festival for both fledgling and established bands to play, and it's amazing how many people have come up through its ranks: Limp Bizkit, Marilyn Manson, Incubus – almost everyone who's any-one in the world of hard rock seems to have played

Ozzfest at some point in their career. What a lot of people don't know is that Dad takes a much smaller cut of the money than he could, just so that the show itself can be improved with bigger and better bands and proper facilities at the gig – but then it was always much more about the music than the money. That's one of the main reasons for its great success.

As a result of being on the road and in that kind of environment, I grew up hanging out with and surrounded by people a lot older than myself. It was something that was to have quite a profound effect on my teenage years, but at the time I completely revelled in it. From when I was quite a little boy, one of my closest friends was Whitfield Crane. Whitfield was the lead singer of a Californian hard-rock band called Ugly Kid Joe; when they split, he went on tour for a while with Life of Agony, then formed a new band, Medication. Whitfield was a hilarious guy – quick-witted, funny, and always up for a laugh. On Ozzfest '98, when I was twelve years old, he was there, touring with Life of Agony, and he became like a big brother to me. It's no coincidence that that was the summer when I *really* started acting out, *really* started learning what I could and couldn't get away with. We would spend all our time together, just fucking around and causing mayhem. It was like that with a lot of the guys in the bands: they knew it was my dad's festival, so if I was with them while they were creating havoc, they knew they wouldn't get into trouble. There was another band on that tour called Snot. Their lead singer was a guy called Lynn Strait – not long afterwards he died in a terrible car crash – and he was another guy with a fantastic sense of humour. Together, Whitfield and Lynn incited all kinds of mischief, with me right next to them.

On that tour, everyone was obsessed with golf carts. The venues for the festivals were so big that you'd need these carts to get from one end to the other. The three of us were constantly stealing these golf carts, riding them to the point of destruction and then destroying them anyway. Anything stupid or juvenile you could do, we did it. And at the time, as a twelve-year-old hanging out with these dudes in their twenties, I thought this was the greatest thing ever; but they were grown men causing all this trouble! I used to go round with a video camera, which I dubbed the official Ozzfest Boobcam, taking home movies of girls flashing me on the camera (later to find out, of course, that some guy went on to earn a million dollars from making those 'girls gone wild' DVDs).

Quite simply, we terrorised the place, and we got away with murder. Every now and then we'd be hauled up in front of the venue security people; they would read us the riot act and then take us to be reprimanded by the head of Ozzfest security. But he would be working for the tour, which meant he worked for my family, so he'd just say, 'Ah, let them go'. Which meant we were free to continue our shenanigans undisturbed.

There was nothing we couldn't do. It was just madness.

At one venue the organisers made the mistake of giving ten bands the same dressing room – a huge locker room at this massive football stadium. It was debauchery. In one corner, Lynn Strait was filming a full-on porno movie; in another there were a couple of tattoo artists giving people tattoos; elsewhere people would be smoking unreasonable quantities of pot and drinking beers; some guys would be playing video games. It was mayhem. I had made friends with a kid called Richie – his step-dad was the lead singer in a huge Brazilian metal band called Sepultura (which he later left to form a new group called Soulfly) – and we were slap bang in the middle of all this stuff going on. All of a sudden, we turned round to see my mum and his mum walk in. I held my breath, not quite sure what kind of trouble I was going to be in; but to my relief, Mum didn't really seem to care. In fact, I seem to remember she just laughed. To be fair, I wasn't really doing any-thing wrong at the time, I was just in there. And although it wasn't really a suitable place for a couple of twelve-year-olds to be hanging out, the truth was that it was all part and parcel of the reality of being on tour – and it was genuinely hilarious.

Limp Bizkit were part of that tour and, as part of their stage set-up, they had this enormous, twelve-foot-high toilet. It had steps at the back, and that's how they'd appear at the start of the gig, coming up through the toilet and then jumping down on stage. When the tour reached Boston, Lynn thought it would be funny to walk up to the top of the toilet during the Limp Bizkit set, stand on the toilet seat and have a girl give him head while they were playing. We all knew this was going to happen, so we found ourselves a good vantage point in the crowd to watch the proceedings. All of a sudden we saw his head appear above the rim of the toilet, then his neck, then his bare chest – it soon became clear to the whole audience that he was completely naked, except for a pair of Converse trainers and some socks hiked all the way up to his knees. Then a girl appears, and she starts blowing him right there for everyone to see.

Immediately you could see all the security guards bounding towards him; then the cops get in on the act and start rushing towards the stage. Lynn saw all this happening, so he ran back down the toilet and started looking for somewhere to hide. He knew there was one place that none of the Ozzfest security guards would dare to go, and that was my dad's dressing room; so Lynn knocks on the door and walks, stark naked apart from his shoes and socks, inside. Dad was just hanging out, watching a movie or something, waiting to go on in six hours' time, and all of sudden this naked, tattoo-covered guy walks in, sits next to him and starts chatting away like it was the most natural thing in the world. Dad knew who Lynn was, of course, and knew he was a troublemaker, but they chatted for a while before he actually got round to asking the question that was on his mind.

'So, er, Lynn. Why are you naked in my dressing room?'

'Ah, you know, the cops are after me . . .' he replies, as if that sort of thing happened every day.

Dad thought he was hilarious, but the cops took a different point of view: Lynn was charged with indecent exposure. Always the joker, on his arrest papers he said that the name of his band was Megadeth. But he died before the case came to court: a tragic death of a genuinely funny guy.

My friend Richie and I were forever blowing things up, setting off fireworks – especially when the tour reached the Midwest, where fireworks are legal and easily available. In that area you get these huge firework supermarkets, and we were like kids in a sweetie shop in those places. We used to make stop-animation films with little figures, and they would always end up being blown to smithereens by some enormous rocket. But our little carton figures weren't the only individuals getting pretty seriously fucked up. There's always some kind of new vehicle trend at Ozzfest. On the '98 tour it was those golf carts; later on the craze turned to mopeds, then it was razor scooters, and latterly it has been these little motorbikes that they make in America. Problem was, of course, that everyone would get absolutely fucked out of their heads and then start riding these vehicles – whatever the flavour of the month was – at a million miles an hour. More often than not they'd end up in a worse state than our blown-up stop-animation characters.

Not all the Ozzfest artists were as crazy as Whitfield and Lynn, or as hard-living as, say, the guys in Pantera, who were nuts – southern metal guys who spent the whole tour at the bottom of a bottle of Crown Royal whisky. I became friendly with Marilyn Manson one year, and soon realised what a sharp, insightful guy he is – probably one of the smartest guys I've ever met. He's incredibly intelligent, incredibly well-spoken, he knows a lot about all different kinds of stuff, and is the sort of person that you can sit and talk to for a very long time. It wasn't that he didn't like to party, but he was never running around doing all these crazy, mental things. He was always able to keep things together, just sitting there sipping tequila while everyone else was losing it all around him.

And while all the craziness was going on, Dad would stay kind of detached from it all. When the partying was happening, he would pop in and perhaps say hello to Marilyn Manson, or the guys in Pantera, all of whom he had known for years. But the truth was that on the whole the bands who played Ozzfest were all full of young guys. Dad had been there and done that twenty years previously, before a lot of them were born, and he definitely set a trend for all the kinds of things that they were doing. All that stuff was boring to him now – he'd

been getting drunk and trashing dressing rooms back in
1972. He'd put all that rock star stuff behind him. It's
only very occasionally that you see him act like a super-
star – normally when he's reached the end of his tether
and has nothing else left to say. Then it will all come out.
'I don't have to do that.'

'Yeah, you do.'

'Fuck off, I don't have to.'

'Why?'

'I can do whatever I want. I'm Ozzy fucking
Osbourne.'

But afterwards, he always feels like a bit of a dick,
because he knows that's not really him. So on tour, the
occasional tantrum aside, he'd really just be pretty laid-
back and let everyone else get on with it.

He'd still have to deal with the fans of course, but on
the whole that was fine. And he had us to help him do
it. By the time Ozzfest had been going for a couple of
years, even though I was by no means a 'celebrity' to the
average Joe, I was pretty well known among the fans
because I had done a couple of weird 'behind the scenes
at Ozzfest' shows for MTV, so I got to realise that for
the most part Dad's fans were pretty cool and respectful.
That's not to say that they weren't wild – you'd always
see those guys running around with no shirts on, getting
drunk, puking in the hedge then passing out in the blazing summer heat – but generally speaking they knew
where to draw the line when it came to giving Dad the
respect he deserved.

Not that there wasn't the occasional weirdo, of
course. Something about the kind of music my dad
plays, and the kind of band that was put on at Ozzfest,
seems to attract them. I found I became pretty proficient
at weeding them out. You learn to recognise the look in

their eyes, the tone of their voice – just something about them that tells you that it would be a good idea to keep your conversation short and sweet. You know that they're going to get round to asking the inevitable question – 'Can I meet your dad?' – so you also learn how to let them down politely but firmly. The last thing Dad wanted was me leading some psycho into his dressing room when he's getting ready for a show. That said, I would do my best to accommodate the fans if I could, even if they might have seemed a bit excessive to somebody not used to seeing what people will do to show their respect for their idols. If someone had a tattoo of my dad on their skin, it might seem a bit odd; but in fact that kind of thing is respectful in a way – it shows a lot of commitment – so maybe I would try to introduce that person to Dad, or get him to sign something for them. At times I used to feel that I was ending up being a bit of a slave to these people, but somewhere deep inside my head the words my mum would constantly tell us kept ringing loud: the fans make us who we are; the fans give us a job; don't ever forget the fans.

And we never did. We still don't. But that didn't mean Dad shouldn't keep himself to himself on Ozzfest, and that's what he did. Truth to tell, I think he pretty much hates working now. Most men his age, who have had a career as long as his, are thinking of retiring now, or at least relatively soon, and I think Dad feels the same way. Whenever his tantrums do occur, they're invariably about work and how he doesn't want to do it. Really he's more of a homebody now, a creature of habit. He likes to do the same thing at the same time every day: eat, work out, watch TV. He does the appointments he has to do, but he doesn't really like going out that much. And if that's how he wants to live for the rest of his life, then why the hell shouldn't he? He's earned it, and it's his life. Because at the end of the day he *is* Ozzy Osbourne. He's been there, done that, bought the T-shirt and ripped it up again. He can do whatever he wants.

THREE

SCHOOL'S OUT

Much as I would have liked it, we couldn't be on tour all the time, and even though Mum and Dad would sometimes let me miss school to go on the road with them, the time would always come when I had to go back to being an ordinary kid. I found school more and more difficult. The dyslexia was certainly one factor. It wasn't like I couldn't read, or that letters looked all back to front or anything; it was more that I would look at a word, and it would just take a while for it to click in my head. The result was, of course, that it took me a long time to read anything, and I had the same trouble with maths. It's something I've inherited from my dad. When he was a kid, he had a horror of being made to stand up and read in front of the class. For me it was exactly the same. Everything academic was a slow, painful struggle.

But it soon became clear to my teachers at the Gateway School in England that there was more to my inability to concentrate in class than that. I'd find my mind wandering all over the place: one minute my attention would be on one thing, the next it would be redirected somewhere totally different, and this was hardly an ideal state of affairs in a school environment. Eventually I was diagnosed with a second learning disorder. Attention Deficit Hyperactivity Disorder, or ADHD, is a condition characterised by inattentiveness and restlessness. It normally appears in children of about the age I was when my symptoms started becoming obvious – ten or eleven – and it manifests itself most often when the child is presented with something that is not especially interesting or potentially rewarding. Once people with ADHD have been distracted from a particular task, they find it difficult to re-engage with that task, and while the disorder tends to diminish as the child makes his or her passage into adulthood, it all spells trouble for somebody at school. In addition to all this, I had a seemingly inexhaustible supply of energy, and nothing to do with it. I couldn't concentrate, and I couldn't sit still. Whereas most kids could be told to sit down and do their homework, my attention would constantly wander, my mind flitting about like a magpie distracted by something shiny.

Slowly but surely my teachers recognised the condition, and I went to a special class two or three times a week to help me deal with it. It was a one-on-one class, and we would do special assignments to help me learn techniques that would enable me to focus more and manage the symptoms of the ADHD – weird shit like putting earplugs in to keep distractions to a minimum, or concentrating on your breathing while you're working. They gave me extra reading to do to help me with that side of things too. And to an extent, I went along with it and tried to practise what was being preached, although that might have had more to do with the fact that the classes coincided with my religious education lessons, which were never something that were very dear to my heart!

When I was eleven, we moved back to Los Angeles.

We weren't living in the Palisades this time, but had rented a house in Beverley Hills that belonged to Don Johnson and Melanie Griffith. Nevertheless, I was enrolled at the same Christian school in the neighbourhood that I had attended last time we had lived in LA. It was now quite a way from where we lived – about a forty-minute drive – but neither I nor my parents had any reason to believe that it wouldn't be as good a place as it had been previously. That first morning when I got dressed in my school uniform, I didn't give the silver cross emblazoned on the white polo shirt we had to wear a second thought. It was going to be the same school I remembered from a few years ago, wasn't it?

I couldn't have been more wrong.

Since I had last been there, the school had come under new administration. It had turned from a nice, sweet place into this really evangelical establishment. I had no problem with the fact that it was a Christian school – that didn't bother me in the slightest. But even at that young age I took exception to the way I felt they were trying to brainwash their kids into acting in certain ways. For a start, we were discouraged from hanging out with anybody who was not a Christian. And as the weeks went by, I started to grow increasingly paranoid that I was hearing things, because I could hardly believe the stuff we were being told. A lot of the kids had been there for such a long time that they didn't really question the school's doctrine, but for me it was a total anathema – I was used to going on the road with the Ozzy Osbourne show, and now I was being told who I could and couldn't spend time with. If only they knew . . .

As the weeks went by, I started rebelling against the whole thing: the system, the teachers, even the pupils themselves. Sure enough, I started to be a bit of an outsider there, and despite all the high-minded religious ideals of the school I became pretty unpopular. The kids started bullying me. Nothing serious – I'd get spat at, and sometimes they would try to fight me in a half-ass kind of way. Fortunately it was the only time I ever got bullied in my whole childhood. People react to that kind of thing in different ways. Some of them withdraw into their shells, hoping that if they stay quiet the bullying will stop; some fight back, taking their battles into the playground and finding themselves getting in more trouble than the people bullying them. Me, I did what seemed natural for me to do: I started rebelling even more.

I wasn't alone. I had a friend who was equally unpopular. His name was Albert, and we would sit together at the back of the class, doing whatever we could to make our contempt for the institution known.

Back in England, my learning disorders – dyslexia and ADHD – had been treated sensibly and responsibly. And in any normal situation, that would have been the case anywhere in America – more so than in the UK, you get cut a bit more slack, afforded a little leniency. In practice, this means you get given extra time in tests, and special help to teach you how to cope with the difficulties you are bound to encounter in the school environment and beyond. I had a whole bunch of documentation stating that I had disabilities, that I needed this extra time and extra care.

And did I get the extra input? Did I fuck. Their solution to my problem was a little more ethereal: pray hard enough and you'll get better. But of course, I didn't get better, and it wasn't because I didn't pray.

I was having such a hard time with my work that I started going to one of those homework clubs. These are provided for kids who are having trouble concentrating on their homework at home, and are held in quiet, library-type settings. The idea is that everyone just sits quietly and does their homework, then leaves when they're done. A nice idea, but it really didn't address the root of my problem: I couldn't focus, and I was totally hyper.

Back in school, my reaction was fairly predictable. I *could* have insisted that my parents kick up a stink. But of course I didn't – I was only eleven years old, after all. I just started to go off the rails.

The first time I got busted for cheating, all hell broke loose. Copying someone else's work just wasn't the sort of thing you did at a school like that; but with the odds stacked against me, and with my utter contempt for the place foremost in my mind, it was kind of inevitable that that was the path I would take. Gradually things started to spiral downwards. Suddenly I found myself being the instigator of all the fights that were happening in the schoolyard; and of course I began to fail miserably at all the classes.

To make matters worse, I started learning that having a famous name could be as much a hindrance as a help. Never in a million years would I have asked for or expected to have any special treatment on account of who my dad was. That way of thinking just wasn't part of my mindset, and even if it was, Mum and Dad would have stamped on it pretty swiftly. But there are always people who believe that you expect special privileges, and in their attempt to make sure you don't get them, they move too far to the other end of the scale and start to discriminate against you. That's just what started to happen with some of the teachers at this school. Suddenly, not ever having wanted my background to give me any kind of advantage over other people, I found it was giving me an actual disadvantage. People assumed that I was just some spoiled rich brat who expected more attention because of who he was, and they treated me all the worse for it. I felt isolated; more than anything else, I felt different.

I stayed at that school for about five months before it became clear to everyone involved that I was as unsuited to the place as a person could possibly be. And then, just as everything was coming to a head, we had one of those convenient moves back across the Atlantic. I said goodbye to the Christian school without a hint of regret.

Back in England, I slotted into my previous school life without any problem at all, as adaptable as always. I caught up with my old friends and enjoyed everything that Welders House and its environs had to offer. But the rot had set in, and my dislike of education seemed now to be pretty much concrete.

We stayed in the UK for a year, then made my final childhood relocation back to Los Angeles. This time there was no question of going back to the Christian school – it was obvious to everyone that it was the last place I should be, and I doubt I'd have been allowed back even if I wanted to go. This time, because of the dyslexia and ADHD, I was enrolled in a special school for children with learning disabilities.

This school was housed in an old warehouse, so it was a pretty small place with probably no more than fifty or sixty pupils there between the ages of six and fifteen. There couldn't have been more than ten other children in my particular age group. It was an expensive school – there were a lot of kids whose dads worked in the stock market, or were investment bankers, property

I think I'd just been born . . . don't really remember.

ADHD boy! That's Aimee on the left and Kelly on the right.
(Tony Mottram)

I still have that bear, 'Baby'.

On a family holiday to Zermatt.
(I had the shits the whole time.)

Beel House where I lived until I was five or six.

I just got back from the great
train robbery.

Dad and I working on our tan in
Maui. That was a good holiday.

Hmmmm . . . I think this is Hawaii still, scene of most family holidays.

We look awesome in leather! This was at Red Rocks Ampitheatre in Colorado. I think we were filming a video. (Mark Leialoha)

Told you I was a weird kid. Taken on Dad's Theatre of Madness tour, 1991–92.

Aimee, Kelly and myself freezing our arses off in the courtyard at Welders.

Kelly and me on Dad's plane in 1997 or 1998.

The Osbourne Clan at Beverly Drive: Aimee, Dad, Louis, Mum, Kelly, Jessica and me! This was taken for Dad's fiftieth birthday.

'No! No! No! No! People are watching!' (Ross Halfin/Idols)

Me, Hannah Wood and Kelly. I live with Hannah now. She's the one who keeps me out of trouble. (This was Hawaii.)

Shit faced!

The most over-used Osbournes picture . . . EVER. Taken to promote
the start of our television series in 2002. (Empics)

developers, lawyers, even basketball players. They
needed to be in high-earning jobs to afford the $25,000-
a-term fees that the place charged, and to be able to field
without blinking the constant requests for millions of
dollars in fundraising However, despite the fact that the
school was exclusively available to those who had a bit
of money, there was no way you could say it was a
warm, cosy kind of place. But it was nurturing: the
teacher to student ratio was pretty high, and so there
was always someone around to help if you ran into
problems of any kind.

The special school could not have been more
different to the Christian school. There was a lot of one-
on-one tutoring going on, and even when there was a
main class, you were basically left to go at your own
pace – to teach yourself, almost. You would be given a
text book for the whole year and told, 'OK, we'd like
you to try and get through this book in your own time,
but don't worry if you don't manage to finish it. It
doesn't matter.' We were expected to do only so much as
we could manage in a day, and if we ran into problems,
or we didn't understand anything, a teacher would be on
hand to explain it to us.

The intention was a good one, and it was certainly a
relief not to have all those teachers on my back every
hour of the day. But naturally, given my inbuilt resistance to all things to do with school, it was only a
matter of time before I started to abuse the trust that
was put in me. Not horribly, and not all the time, but bit
by bit I learned what I could get away with if I was
to achieve my desired end at school: to do as little as
possible.

Unlike the previous place, I found that I was a great
deal more popular here. The bullying was a thing of the

past and, on the outside at least, my confidence started
to grow. Lots of the kids around me had behavioural
issues that were different to mine – it wasn't all just
dyslexia and ADHD. They also had social issues, emotional issues. I don't know exactly what was wrong with
half of them, but I do know what the net result was: a
lot of the people around me were just downright weird.
Not rowdy in any way – in fact they were more subdued
than anything – but I felt like I was a little more switched
on than all of them. I suppose it was because of my
background, because of the fact that I'd spent time on
the road on tour with Mum and Dad, that I just had the
impression that I was a little more street-smart than
them. I knew how to take the initiative, and I knew how
to handle myself in mature situations that these kids had
never even heard about, let alone experienced – the sort
of thing, I suppose, that no school could ever teach.

And most importantly, I knew how to have a good
time.

But there was one thing that unified us all. One thing
that nearly everybody at that school had in common –
and which accounted for the fact that my classmates
were a good deal less boisterous than I was used to. That
thing was called Ritalin, and I started to take it at the
age of thirteen.

Ritalin is an amphetamine-like stimulant that is used
to treat ADHD. It is also prescribed for people with
narcolepsy and chronic fatigue syndrome, but more than
seventy-five per cent of its usage is for children with
ADHD. Now, I don't know whose idea it first was to
give a hyperactive kid what amounts to pharmaceutical
speed, but that's what they did – and they still don't
quite know why it works. ADHD is caused by a chemical imbalance that is somehow counterbalanced by the

introduction of a stimulant into the body. So instead of giving you the usual effects of a dose of speed, it makes you docile and focused, reduces impulsive behaviour and helps you concentrate on tasks that you previously had difficulty with. Some people abuse the drug by crushing it into a powder and snorting it – it can give a similar effect to that of cocaine or speed, and can lead to addiction. In properly prescribed doses it is non-addictive and doesn't give a high, but there is research that suggests that kids prescribed Ritalin at an early age have a higher chance of succumbing to addictions in later life. A large body of opinion believes that Ritalin is hugely over-prescribed, especially in America; others think it's a wonder drug. I certainly felt it having an effect when I started taking it. The physical symptoms are rather strange: you feel your heart racing, but at the same time you come over feeling very mellow. Certainly it chilled me out a bit, and had some effect on my hyper-active behaviour.

There were plenty of reasons why I was happy to go on Ritalin. The first of these was my weight. At about that time, I had started to realise that I was heavier than a lot of the other kids at school. It wasn't a major problem, but it was something I had noticed, and clearly other people had noticed it too, although it certainly wasn't something that I was given a hard time about. If it was mentioned by my school friends at all, then it would be nothing more than light-hearted and jocular: they'd call me a fat bastard, and I'd tell them that their mum was fucking the gardener! (Which, in the case of one of my schoolmates, happened to be true.) All good clean childhood fun. But despite that, I knew that Ritalin acted as an appetite suppressant, so while I wasn't in any way obsessed about my weight, I do remember thinking that if I could lose a few pounds as a result of it, then there was no reason to be reluctant about taking it. The second reason why I was cool about being on Ritalin was that it was the norm – everyone else at school seemed to be taking it and I guess I felt a bit more in the clique with the other kids on account of the drug.

But the main reason I was perfectly happy to be prescribed the drug was quite different. It wasn't just because I thought I legitimately needed it, that I would benefit from it and be better able to deal with my inability to concentrate; it was quite simply that it gave me an excuse for my problems. I had started to manipulate my teachers, to play up to them and use my learning disabilities as a way of getting out of doing what I didn't want to do. For a while it worked. The phrases 'I'm sorry, I think I have ADHD' and 'I think I need to go on Ritalin' can be pretty effective in a school where everyone is acknowledged as having a learning disorder of some sort. Sometimes it didn't work – there were still teachers here who didn't really take a shine to me, and who thought I expected to be treated differently because of my background. When that happened, I would try to kill them with kindness, to be as polite, charming and witty as I possibly could. I didn't really think that was what I was doing at the time, but looking back I can see how manipulative I was. I was forever pulling the learning-disabled card. 'I just can't focus. I have trouble with this, trouble with that. I read real slow.' It was bullshit, but I knew I could get away with it, and the fact that I had been prescribed Ritalin just added weight to my justifications. Sometimes it would work, sometimes it wouldn't; when it didn't you just had to give up, because ultimately there was no winning.

Gradually my manipulations started being less and less successful. The excuses started to run out – I guess they had heard them all before. But if you don't want to work, you don't want to work – it's as simple as that – and so I simply started skipping a lot of school, or turning up late. As had always been the case, my parents weren't so strict about making me attend, so all credit to the school itself: they put their foot down and did what they could to stop me playing truant. They forced me to start making up for the hours that I had missed, which meant turning up for school at seven in the morning and not leaving until seven at night for about two months. It was a pretty good idea, I suppose, and under other circumstances they might have had some kind of success.

But not with me, because Ritalin wasn't the only substance I was taking at the time. On my thirteenth birthday, I discovered the joys of drinking.

FOUR

TEENAGE KICKS

For as long as I can remember, I've been hanging out with people older than myself. I was close friends with Whitfield Crane at the age of six, and spending so much time in the distinctly adult world of a touring rock band meant that, while I was growing up, I was always comfortable with grown-up company. And while I wasn't an outsider at the special school, I didn't really spend a great deal of time socialising with the people there. Because of all the terrible social and emotional issues they had to deal with, most of them just weren't on my wavelength – by which I suppose I mean they were just too downright weird for my liking.

At around this time Kelly had a tutor who used to give her extra lessons after school and who I became quite friendly with. His name was Louis and his family was from somewhere in Latin America – El Salvador, I think. He looked like some kind of beatnik revolutionary – crazy Afro hair, straggly beard, pale skin. And he was one of the nicest, coolest guys I had ever met. He was really into the arts: he played jazz, he was into painting, and he wrote for a bunch of LA newspapers, as well as tutoring kids like my sister. Louis taught me a lot about the world: he made me think about stuff I had never thought about, and told me about things I had never seen. It was thanks to him that my transition to living permanently in LA was relatively easy. I'd arrived in the city hardly knowing anyone, and all of a sudden I had someone to look out for me. He introduced me to a whole group of new people; perhaps more importantly, he told me who I should stay away from.

Louis was involved with the University of Central Los Angeles, and he was part of an independent theatre group called Lost Dog that was based at the university itself. As I started spending a bit of time with him, he soon took me along to meet the group. There were about twenty-five of them, all students or graduates of UCLA, all with a passion for putting on theatre wherever and whenever they could. They produced all kinds of stuff, from Shakespeare through to modern plays, and were a bit underground – this was as far away from being a big money-making operation as it was possible to be. Certainly nobody got paid – we were just in it to have as much fun as we could. When the performances came round, maybe forty of fifty people would turn up to watch us – including my mum and dad, on occasion.

They would put on their plays wherever they could find the space – converted garages, band-rehearsal spaces, anywhere really that had a place that could act as a stage and had enough room for a small audience. And before I knew it, I was doing plays with them, and I loved every minute. What twelve-year-old wouldn't enjoy hanging out with these guys who were all in their twenties, and playing all the kid roles in their productions? Our biggest event was performing *Julius Caesar*, and I played Brutus's servant Lucius. I revelled in it – even if the language wasn't quite what I was used to at home – it was certainly more poetic than the general conversations that were to be heard around our Los Angeles house.

In addition to the regular productions, we would perform what are known as LARPs (live-action role-playing games). We would decide on a general theme – maybe *Star Trek* or westerns or medieval times – and then a general story line. Maybe a war would be brewing, and the two sides are quarrelling and eventually there's going to be a big battle; or you're on a spaceship, about to land on an alien planet. Next you start to write the basic characters – the king or the cowboy or the knight or the hooker, whatever it might be, and assign a character to each of the actors, who will have to be this character for the whole evening. Each character is given a mission, some sort of goal they have to achieve – maybe the knight of the realm has to win over the heart of the dusky maiden – which nobody else knows about. And that's all there is to it. We would go all over the place acting out our improvised stories for nobody's enjoyment but our own. Needless to say, it was a complete blast.

For a short while I was bitten by the bug. When *The Osbournes* became successful, I started getting offers for parts in movies, but even before then I occasionally found myself turning up to auditions. One of those was for a part in the third Austin Powers movie. A friend of mine worked at the casting agent's office, and she knew that one of my hidden talents was to be able to do a pretty passable Dr Evil impersonation. She persuaded me to audition for the part of the young Dr Evil. In the end it came down to a choice between me and this other guy, but he pipped me to the post by being able to impersonate Austin Powers as well. He got the gig, but I ended up in the movie anyway, along with the rest of the family. In Los Angeles, everyone wants to be an actor, apart from the actors themselves – they all want to be rock stars. When the acting offers began to come in more regularly, I started wondering if I really wanted to be like everybody else. I'd turn up to a few auditions, and it was always the ones for which I did absolutely no preparation that seemed to go the best; those that I studied really hard for would go shit. I didn't much like the auditioning process in any case. I still don't – I can't shake off the feeling that I'm constantly being judged. But I would play around with the few parts that I got – I ended up on *Dawson's Creek* for a weekend, but that was little more than a pay cheque – but my heart wasn't really in it. Maybe in the future it's something I'll do more of, but if I'm honest with myself I would have to say that it would need to fall straight into my lap – it's not like I'm ever going to go out and take acting classes.

So back in the Lost Dog days, I guess it was really more the fact that it was such a lot of fun that attracted me to the process than a genuine desire to tread the boards. And I loved the feeling, of course, of being part of something. I felt comfortable among my new friends – more comfortable than I could ever feel with my schoolmates. I liked the way they treated me as an adult. As it happened, my thirteenth birthday coincided with the birthdays of three of the other guys in the group, so we held this big party. Naturally, there was alcohol there. I was able to get my hands on a few shots of whiskey: unlike most people, I quite liked my first taste, and I got drunk for the first time.

I was always one of those kids who would get paranoid that someone would find out if I did something wrong. I constantly felt the need to cover my tracks, to deny everything. There was no real reason why Mum

and Dad should have found out about my birthday
antics: I had got home late and they were in bed when I
sneaked in; moreover, they fully trusted the people I was
with. But somehow I became obsessed with the idea that
they would. They'll know, I told myself. I don't know
how, but somehow they'll know. Someone's going to
bust me – it's just a matter of time. And I knew how
much it would upset my mum: what with Dad's drinking problem and the fact that alcohol abuse had had
such a huge effect on our family over the years, it would
no doubt have broken her heart to see her thirteen-year-
old son drunk on whiskey.

So, just as a result of that overwhelming sense of
paranoia, I didn't get drunk for quite a while. Maybe I'd
have a beer here, a beer there, but for a few months it
didn't really seem to me to be all that appealing. But,
like all teenagers, I started to learn something about
what I could and couldn't do, and I started wanting to
stretch my boundaries a little. Add to that, of course, the
fact that I was used to getting away with all kinds of
stuff when we were on tour with Dad, and I suppose it
was only a matter of time before I started acting out a
bit more.

I was well used to seeing alcohol and drugs. Not only
had I grown up with it as a result of my dad's addictions,
they were part and parcel of life on the road. You just
couldn't escape them because most of the time half the
bands were drunk or high and they would be doing this
stuff, quite blatantly, right there in front of me. There
was nothing mysterious to me about booze or weed, and
gradually my paranoia at what my parents' attitude
would be if I started using them was replaced by good,
old-fashioned teenage rebellion. As I reached the age of
fourteen, I started drinking on a more regular basis –

once a month, maybe, at friends' houses. And I started smoking pot, too. The first time was at the house of a friend in Hollywood. He was a lot older than me – in his twenties – and I guess I kind of looked up to him. He was one of those guys who really talked the talk: he had led a crazy life. He was cool; he seemed to have it all going on. So I was round there one day and he rolled a joint. Quite nonchalantly, as if it was the most natural thing in the world, he passed it over to me. 'You want a hit?' he asked.

I shrugged. 'Sure,' I told him. I mean, why not? Everyone else I hung out with seemed to be smoking it, and it looked like they all had a pretty good time as a result.

I've never really been one for doing things by halves. That first time I took a drag on a joint, it wasn't just a tentative little puff. There was no dipping my little toe into the water just to see if I liked it; I dive-bombed in and made as big a splash as I could. I inhaled as much and as deeply as I could, and I got high as a kite.

My overwhelming memory of that first time is just that it was totally weird. I sat on the sofa and simply let all the chaos that was happening in the apartment around me unfold. My friend had these big dogs that were prowling all over the place; somewhere in the background there was a band practising, and even though it was quite a way away, I could hear every note with perfect clarity. Everything seemed to be happening at a different kind of pace. Disorientating. Strange.

I hated it. Absolutely, one hundred per cent hated it.

I don't think the fact that I was far from enamoured by the weed was anything unusual. After all, if people's smoking habits were based on their first experience of trying a cigarette, the tobacco companies would go out of business; and there can't be that many kids who can honestly say they really enjoyed their first ever mouthful of beer. After that first time, I didn't touch weed for probably a couple of months, because I just assumed I didn't like it. But then I found myself somewhere – I don't remember the exact occasion – and the stuff was being passed round again. Fuck it, I thought. I've already done it once. Maybe it will be better this time.

And it was.

Even then I did not throw myself wholeheartedly into the pot-smoking lifestyle. Just as it was with my alcohol consumption, I found myself doing it once in a blue moon. Then it started becoming a bit more regular – once every two weeks, perhaps. Then every weekend.

Mum had always encouraged us to be open and honest with her about what we were up to. Both she and Dad were of the opinion that we shouldn't be banned from doing stuff, we should just be advised, given all the facts, and then left to make our own decisions. After all, they had both made their own way in life, made their own choices, and it would be a strange kind of example for us if they had then started coming on all authoritarian. But I knew, nevertheless, that it would be a bad idea to come clean about the fact that I had started using pot and alcohol. In any case, it wasn't like it was a big deal – a few beers and an occasional joint round at someone's house.

It wasn't as if I was a major junkie.

It wasn't as if I was out of control.

The more I started partying, the more my interest in school became sidelined. I just wasn't interested – there were far more exciting and fun things out there to get me fired up, and one of those was music.

I had always known that Dad was a musician, of course, but it wasn't until I became a teenager that I actually started respecting him as such. I began to listen to his music, and that turned me on to all kinds of other stuff – mostly metal and hard rock, the sort of thing I had grown up surrounded by. As time went on, I started expressing my opinion of what was good and what wasn't to Mum. I like to think that I have a pretty good ear for these things, and Mum and I found that we saw eye to eye on a lot of stuff like that. So when it came to booking bands for Ozzfest, she would seek out my opinion. I think the way she saw it was that, as a teenager, I had my finger on the pulse much more firmly than she could ever have: if bands were attractive to her and not to me, they were probably pushing the wrong buttons for the kind of show we wanted to put on. So we would sit around, listen to all the stuff that was under consideration and, if we agreed that we liked it, we would book them – and if we didn't, we wouldn't.

There were exceptions, of course. Sometimes relations within the industry dictated which bands we could promote – if we had a good relationship with some record label and they wanted to put their new metal band on, it would have been bad business sense to say no. But on the whole we were pretty true to what we believed was good, and the Ozzfest shows were better for it.

I seemed to have a knack for knowing what was going to be hot – some of the bands I put in on Ozzfest are still going to this day – and at the time I was keen to start a career in the record industry. It was in the blood, I suppose. So while I may not have had any interest in my schooling, I was fired up enough about the music business to try and do something about it. When I had just turned fourteen, Mum was managing the band Smashing Pumpkins for a stint. It's a brief moment in history that I don't think she looks back on particularly fondly, and it was soon to end pretty acrimoniously. My mum's press release in which she announced that she and the band had decided to go their separate ways was characteristically robust: 'I've resigned from Smashing Pumpkins' management due to medical conditions. Billy Corgan makes me sick.' But before they went their separate ways, Mum was sitting with the marketing people from Virgin, the Pumpkins' label, and I was with her. We were talking about music in general, and I was just chatting along like I always did. Out of the blue they made me an offer. 'Hey, Jack, you want to come and work for us?'

What kind of question was that? I was fourteen, I wanted to be in the music business. Sure I wanted to come and work for them. And so it was that I started my internship for Virgin Records. A lowly position, and no money, but I dug it.

I didn't stay with Virgin for long. Dad had been on Sony Music's Epic label for years at this point, and we had a really good relationship with them. A guy named Steve Barnett, who had been a friend of Mum's since they were teenagers, was really high up on the label, and before long I found myself interning for them instead. They wanted me to do A&R scouting for them. Artists and Repertoire for a major label: going out there and finding local and nationwide talent and bringing it to the label's attention. It sounded pretty grand, and I really took to my new role. I would go to the label a couple of times a week after school, straight from lessons to the

office and into meetings. A few nights a week I'd go
to shows at rock clubs in LA, check out the bands, and
that was about all there was to it – I was basically just
having fun.

The idea behind having someone like me there was a
good one: they needed a young person, someone who
knew what was happening with new music. They were
all much older, and didn't really know what was going
on in the rock scene any more, so they relied on me to
bring new stuff to them. The truth was, of course, that
I was totally blagging it: it didn't really involve much
other than listening to a bunch of music, deciding whether
you liked it, and then thinking, Ah well, maybe they'll
like it too. But blagging or not, they seemed to value my
opinion. A year or so into my internship they started
paying me for my time, and I stayed with them until I
was eighteen years old.

I relished the time I spent scouting for Epic, even
though at times it could be frustrating. Working on
Ozzfest gave us a great deal more autonomy – if we liked
a band, we put them on. The record label, though, was
a much more massive operation, a very corporate company. I would find bands that were really cool, bring
them to label's attention and often they'd seem keen at
first. But then someone high up would start prevaricat-
ing, we'd wait too long and then we'd lose the band to
someone else. By contrast, they'd pick up some group
that were a load of shit and sign them overnight, and I'd
be left wondering what the hell was going on.

It was by no means always on account of the record
label that certain bands didn't fulfil their potential. I
found this one group and they were put on a development deal. This is basically a situation whereby the label
give a band a bunch of money in the hope that they will

get good by practising every day, recording a load of stuff and hopefully coming up with something that could be released as an EP or some other kind of finished product. These guys were really cool when I first came across them. They came from the Valley, from the same area as the guys in the band Incubus, who I had got to know through Ozzfest, and I had really high hopes for them. But I grew to learn that a strange thing happens a lot with bands: as soon as they get the interest of a record label, they tend to lose sight of what it is that they were trying to become in the first place. They lose their way. It's kind of disappointing, not only for them when they learn that you're not going to follow through on the development deal, but also for the people who have put so much time and effort into trying to make it work. But I learned to accept the fact that it was part and parcel of being in the record industry – it's a hard business to survive in, and getting a taste of it made me respect my mum and dad even more for what they had achieved.

But despite the frustrations, I was having a ball. I was really pretty young when I started hanging out at the major rock clubs in Los Angeles – the Roxy, the Troubadour, the Whiskey, the Palladium, the Viper Room – all the famous places down Sunset Strip that were where all the exciting new bands were playing. More to the point, I started getting a taste for the LA club scene.

You spend all summer hanging out with adults, and not just any adults – adults who really like to have a good time. You're on the road, you move from one city to another, surrounded by the craziness and the debauchery of a travelling rock show. Maybe you have a few drinks

– who cares that you're only fourteen? – and you certainly do a lot of partying. It doesn't take a rocket scientist to work out that when you get back home, when the whirlwind of the summer is over, you're going to want to carry on the party.

I was drinking more and more; I was smoking more and more. I had also become friends with a guy who was managing bands, and he owned a bar in Hollywood. He told me I could turn up there whenever I wanted, and he made sure all the security guys and bartenders knew who I was. So by the time I was fifteen, I had become aware of the fact that Los Angeles is a place where exceptions are made because of who you are: I could turn up at this bar whenever I wanted to, order a drink and get drunk. It's pretty appealing at that age, and it started to happen rather a lot.

It's amazing the confidence that a thing like that can give you. On the outside, I was all bravado, oozing self-assertiveness and able to hold up a conversation with anybody I met. But self-confidence so often hides something else – a social anxiety that you feel the need to smother in some way – and when I look back I realise that was the case with me. If you go into a hip club in LA, you'll see that all the celebrities have a table of their own, with a bottle of booze for them and their entourage, and everyone will flock to them. It's like they all have their own little scene going on in the corner. Even if you're not a celebrity, they can be pretty cliquey kinds of places. If that's not part of the way you are, as it isn't with me, it can be pretty daunting to see these groups from whom you are so obviously excluded. I would turn up at these places, and although I would successfully be able to put on a show of being incredibly sociable – thanks to a bit of liquid courage – deep down

I was always aware of the fact that I was just a fifteen-year-old kid, about the height of the bar, and not really fitting in with any of the groups of people around me. It's something that has stuck with me to this day: whenever I go out to a bar, a pub or a club with a group of friends, I always feel that we are different to all the others around us. It can be a pretty uncomfortable sensation, feeling that you're being looked down on all the time, and back when I was fifteen there seemed to be only one way to deal with it: more alcohol.

Everyone else seemed to be drinking beers and shots of tequila – it was what was fashionable at the time – so I joined in. The booze made me feel good, but more importantly it made me feel relaxed, more able to enjoy myself. And the more I enjoyed myself, the more I wanted to go out. I was a teenager having fun – there was nothing wrong with that – and in many ways, I suppose, I wasn't a whole lot different to most other normal kids my age, kids for whom partying was just part of growing up. But at the time, I felt different. Maybe it was because I wasn't really hanging out with the kids from my school; or maybe it was because they and I were as different as chalk and cheese. Their parents were all millionaire bankers. Their dads were all very white-collar, they played golf every Sunday, they watched the game; maybe – just maybe – they drank a Bud Lite; their mums were the archetypal rich Californian wives with big tits, blonde hair and not much to do with their time. I was the exception to every rule at that place. When I turned up to classes on a Monday morning, they'd ask me what I got up to at the weekend. 'Ah, you know,' I would say. 'I went to this bar, got completely drunk. It was crazy.' And almost without exception, they could hardly believe what they were hearing. If I'd been at an ordinary high school, no doubt I'd have been one of many. But not there. In comparison to the people at the special school, I was an absolute lunatic.

My reputation was enhanced by the fact that the guys from the LA band System of a Down, who were pretty well known at the time, occasionally used to pick me up from school. They would pull up in front of the school buildings in an old white Bronco with clouds of smoke billowing out of the window. They took me under their wing, and the drummer, John, used give me the occasional lesson in chatting up women. Between him and Whitfield, I had a well-rounded education in affairs of the heart!

I was unlike my schoolmates in another respect, too: I had more money in my pocket than them. Although none of them came from anything other than very rich backgrounds, they led much more structured lives than I did, and as a result did not need to have the same kind of pocket money I was given. From the age of fourteen, I started getting $200 a week. It sounds like a lot for a young teenager, I know, but I found it alarmingly easy to get through. Somehow $200 doesn't get you very far when you are travelling everywhere by taxi, buying lunch for school, eating dinner at restaurants with friends in the evening, going out and getting drunk and then buying weed occasionally. Unlike my contemporaries, these were all things that I was doing on a more or less regular basis – I was a very independent teenager.

Also unlike my contemporaries, I had no trouble talking to girls. Don't forget that I had been almost exclusively raised by women, so there was no stage in my life when I felt uncomfortable in their presence. And

I suppose it didn't help that I spent so much of my early life hanging out with guys in their twenties who were just the most massive womanisers in the world. You can't be around people like that when they are in full-on party mode and not learn how to talk to girls in the right way. The first time I kissed a girl was when I was eight – one of Aimee's friends – and it was fantastic. When I reached thirteen or fourteen, I was spending increasing amounts of time in their company, and it was just another thing that gave me a certain cachet among my classmates. Hanging out in bars! Drinking! With girls! No way!

One of the things that Mum has always insisted on, though, and it has stuck with me throughout my life and into adulthood, is that I should talk about and treat women with respect. She's always had something to say about the kind of guy that brags about how many women he's fucked and what he did to them, and I've always agreed with her that it somehow makes the whole thing seem cheap and hollow. My love life is something that I've never wanted to talk about, to go into any kind of detail on, and that's not about to change. Suffice to say that I've never had a serious, long-term girlfriend, and I've never been in love. It's not that I don't want a serious relationship, but I find it difficult to stay focused on one girl for long enough. I've been with lots of beautiful women, but somehow I always manage to find fault with them. It's a defect in myself that I hate. Nevertheless, I always seem to have been popular with girls – and all that entails. I don't want to pretend that I didn't enjoy it, and the more I partied, the more I drank and the more I smoked weed, the more popular I seemed to become. Slowly but surely I was becoming addicted, to alcohol certainly, but to some-

thing else too: I was addicted to fun. I would do anything for a good time.

Every Friday and Saturday night, I would find myself at
a bar in LA. I'd hang out, have a few drinks and a good
time. I'd sometimes bump into the guys from Incubus –
this was when they were at their height – and it would
always be pretty mellow, nothing really to worry about.
Apart from one thing: the old paranoia would kick in
when it was time to leave. For fuck's sake, I would think
to myself. I've been drinking, and I hope to hell Mum
doesn't realise.

But of course it's hard to hide the fact that you're
drunk, and my folks cottoned on to what I was doing
pretty quickly. I would get bollocked for it the next day,
but once that's happened three or four times, it tends
to lose its effect. Perhaps more to the point, my mum
began to accept that maybe I was just doing what
teenagers do. And that was true – I was being carefree
and having harmless fun. Eventually, Mum told us that
she didn't have a problem with us drinking. She wasn't
wildly happy about us doing it, but she would much
rather know everything we were up to and not have to
guess all the time, or force it out of us. She told us never
to try to drive when we were drunk, or be driven by
someone who was, but otherwise she said she was cool
about it.

Saying it is one thing; meaning it is another. I knew
even then that Mum was incredibly scared that I would
end up like my dad when it came to alcohol, so as I
started partying harder and harder, I did my best to hide
from her the extent of it. It wasn't easy. Los Angeles is a
small town in many ways, and my mum and dad were

well known. Everywhere I went out drinking I would bump into people who knew them, which did nothing for my sense of paranoia! I would drink nine or ten tequilas, then just as many beers and end up vomiting in the street, and I knew that my mum would get a phone call from somebody who had seen it all happen. It was pretty difficult to pull the wool over her eyes. I'd get home at night and quick as a flash she would ask me how much I'd had to drink.

'Nothing, Mum.'

'Nothing?'

'Well, maybe one beer?'

'Just one beer?'

'And a couple of tequilas . . .'

Soon enough she would work out the truth about how much I'd had. Sometimes I'd be in trouble; sometimes she would take it in her stride. When she did lose it with me, I'd make an effort to back off for a bit, to take it easy. But sooner rather than later I'd be hard at it again. It was just too much fun not to.

One of the best places in the world that I know to have fun is Malibu. Our family owns a house there nowadays, but back then we used to rent places on the beachfront. They would always be pretty big, with wide open spaces, massive decks, and all the deck furniture and barbecues you need to have a fabulous time. You could just walk down a ladder and you'd be on the beach; walk ten feet and you'd be in the water. In the summertime especially, it's the greatest place on the planet, and I had some genuinely amazing times there that I couldn't have experienced in any other way. I would have friends round, and we would spend all day on the beach in the glaring sun. We'd invite girls over, have a bit of pot, a bit of booze and just start partying.

Those parties would carry on late into the night; the next day I would wake up, the same crowd would still be there, and we would just carry on.

My life was turning into one long rave, and I didn't want it to end.

I wasn't the only one of the Osbourne brood that was discovering that Los Angeles was our oyster. Aimee was always much more anti-drugs and alcohol than me, but the same couldn't be said for Kelly. Not by a long chalk. One day Kelly came home and in her typical 'Oh, I'm such a lunatic' kind of way threw a rock at Aimee's window and cracked the glass. Aimee was furious. She stormed out of the house. 'What the fuck is wrong with you?'

One look at Kelly would have told anyone. 'I totally just smoked pot,' she boasted.

Aimee's first reaction was kind of predictable. She went straight to Mum's room and told her. 'Kelly's high.'

Cue the fireworks. Mum went absolutely ballistic. She stormed out of her room and started screaming. 'What the fuck have you been doing?' she yelled at Kelly.

It was typical Kelly, drawing attention to herself; but when she confessed, Mum went completely on the war-path. She called the school, she called the parents of everyone that Kelly was with. I guess this was what she had always been terrified of. Alcohol was one thing, but the idea of her kids following their father down the path of drug use must have absolutely ripped her apart.

Kelly was taking so much flak that day, and I couldn't really understand what the big deal was – all she had done was get high, like any number of other teenagers experimenting with what was available to them – so I thought I would try to ease some of the weight of Mum's displeasure away from her. The family was all together, so now was as good a time as any to come clean. 'Actually, Mum,' I confessed, 'I smoke pot too.'

The reaction wasn't quite what I had expected. Maybe it was because I wasn't high at the time, but I seemed to get off more lightly than Kelly. Now, though, it was out in the open, no secret in the family that I drank and smoked weed.

From that moment, there was a change in Mum and Dad's relationship. It suddenly became more volatile, more argumentative. They've always argued of course. Like all married couples, they have their disagreements. Even now, every eighteen months or so, they'll have some big fucking row and won't talk to each other for days on end. But at that particular time it seemed a bit more serious. She had always respected us enough to let us make our own choices, and now it seemed to be backfiring on her. I wouldn't necessarily say that Mum needed somebody to blame for our behaviour, but perhaps in her head she needed to justify why we were going down that path. The most obvious reason was the one closest at hand. I don't think she ever went so far as to say to Dad, 'Look what you've done now', but she wasn't far off.

As for me, I never worried at that time about the amount of weed and alcohol I was using. It wasn't controlling me. It wasn't going to lead to anything more serious. I could quit at any time.

Or so I thought . . .

FIVE

PHARMACOPOEIA

At that time, there were two sides to Jack Osbourne.

In fact, looking back, there always had been. As a child, there had always been a destructive streak in my nature, and it used to manifest itself in different ways. One of those was an obsession with fire. I was always acting out with it as a kid, to the point that I would walk out into the woods around Welders House in England with the express intention of setting fire to my toys, or to cans of gas – anything remotely combustible. I got burned a few times, and would walk back into the house with the front of my hair singed, my eyelashes and eyebrows scorched. Dad would look at me like I was some kind of fucking idiot, and occasionally he would yell at me. And trust me: he may seem like a docile person, but when Dad yells, he really yells. The whole house would shake in its foundations – being screamed at by him was not something to look forward to.

More often than not, though, his reprimands would be of a very different nature. He knew that because of everything he had done in his life, it was hard for him to give me a really hard time. So he would just sit me down and say, 'Look, Jack. I can't sit here and yell at you, and tell you not to do these things, because I'd be such a hypocrite as I did them myself. Just use your common sense. Remember that there's a consequence to every action – whether it's a good one or a bad one. Don't ever forget that.'

A consequence to every action. It was clever. He left the ball in my court, letting me know that he trusted me to be as sensible as I possibly could. So when I fucked up, I would feel guilty that I had disappointed him, that I had abused the trust that he had put in me.

It didn't stop me from fucking up, though.

From the moment I became a teenager, I started having trouble controlling my temper. It's difficult to say what caused all the feelings of anger that welled up inside me, but I guess they were largely caused by insecurity – as with most teenagers. I had these raging hormones and things were changing. I used to have short, straight hair; all of a sudden I wake up one day and it's this big curly afro. I started gaining more and more weight. I was self-conscious. Truth to tell, I started somewhat hating myself.

Family-wise, things were going downhill, too. There was a lot of arguing, and Aimee, Kelly and I always seemed to be fighting – we seemed to fucking hate the sight of each other at the time. Kelly and Aimee would beat the shit out of one another; Kelly and I would beat the shit out of one another; Aimee would push Mum around; Mum would push Dad around; there were always fights going on. It was like a war zone, and I knew it wasn't normal, which made me feel incredibly frustrated, and a lot of the anger I had started to feel came out of that frustration.

I would have these incredible fits of rage. I'd trash my room and get into really nasty, vicious fistfights with my sisters. I think the tipping point for my parents came when I held a knife to Kelly's throat. To be honest, I can't even remember why I did it – it was just a result of this terrible anger that was bubbling under the surface. In an attempt to keep it under control, I started taking antidepressants. It was Mum who brought the issue up – it was clear to her that all was not well, so she suggested to my therapist that something should be done. I made the final decision to start taking them, though – a kind of tacit acknowledgement that I was miserable. I had stopped taking Ritalin after I had seen some programme on TV suggesting it was over-prescribed, and as a result my schoolwork had gone well and truly down the pan, but I needed something else to manage the anger I was experiencing. But I would only take the antidepressant pills for a few weeks before I would run out, be too lazy to go and get a new prescription, and just think, Fuck it. The depression started to grab a tighter hold on me, and the anger didn't go away.

I didn't want to take Ritalin, and I didn't want to take antidepressants. I knew of a much easier way to make the anger disappear: go down to the Rainbow and hang out with a bunch of rockers and porn stars. Drink. Smoke. For a fifteen-year-old, that was the life.

The teachers at the special school had other ideas, of course. From almost as soon as I started there, they suggested that I should go into therapy. They said that they found a lot of the kids benefited from it – in fact I think it was just part of their format, the way they liked to do things. As I've said, a lot of the kids there were different in some way – different enough, at least, for them not to have to go to a normal school – and it was believed that therapy was a good way for them to talk about how they felt about being different. They were probably right. Certainly I liked going to therapy, having someone to talk to about all the shit that was going on in my life. I still see this guy, occasionally. He's fantastic, and I like the feeling that everything you tell him is locked away deep in this secret dungeon, where nobody else can find out about it.

Back then, however, I was never a hundred per cent honest with him. Part of that stemmed from my paranoia – I didn't ever really feel that I could be a hundred per cent honest about anything with *any* adult. He knew about the drink, and the drugs, and as my using started to get heavier and more out of control, he knew about that too – it was difficult to hide it, after all. But it did feel weird talking to an adult about absolutely everything, like the girls and the sex. Uncomfortable. More to the point, as I was under eighteen, I knew that my parents had a perfect right to call him up and ask questions about what we had been discussing. And they did that a lot, especially when they learned that I had started getting high. I would turn up to a therapy session and he'd be perfectly straight with me about it. 'Your mother called me the other day, and asked me a few questions.'

I had a hard time dealing with that at first. 'What the fuck's that all about?' I remember asking him, my hackles rising.

'It's the law. You're not eighteen, so nothing that is said here is completely confidential. I'm not going to openly give things away, but if your mother asks me specific questions, I have to answer her.'

So I started to edit myself. That's not to say I didn't get a lot out of it. I did, but I really didn't want her to find out too many details about certain things – the sex, and especially the alcohol and the drugs, both of which were moving up to a different level of consumption.

It had just been the weed to start with; but as I started getting more and more into the club scene in Los Angeles, I became aware of the fact that a lot of my friends were using a drug called Vicodin. Vicodin – or hydrocodone, to give it its generic name – is an opiate-based painkiller that is widely prescribed in America. Its recreational use is equally prevalent, though, and you can pretty much walk into any bar in LA and ask for a Vicodin in the same way as you might ask for a cigarette – people will fish into their bags and hand you one like they're handing you a stick of gum. If you look in the medical dictionaries, they will tell you that hydrocodone relieves pain by binding itself to the opioid receptors in the brain and spinal cord. If you're looking for a hit, what that basically means is that it gets you really high and really dopey. In the past, it had been one of the pills that I had seen my Dad swallowing – the ones that had made me want to go and buy a box of Tic-Tacs just to be like him. Now I saw my friends going out, having a few drinks and dropping a Vicodin. I knew that if you mixed it with alcohol, the effects were enhanced, and I wanted to find out what it was like.

I was staying with a friend in the Beverley Hills Hotel – a kind of home from home for my family. I had been hanging out with this girl quite a lot, and we decided to take a Vicodin. I really, really liked it. It made me feel comfortable, I suppose, and I had always dug that kind of dopey, not-really-too-aware-of-what's-going-on feeling. (I already had a habit, whenever we had cans of whipped cream in the fridge, of sucking out the nitrous oxide to give me that spaced-out sensation.) This girl and I just spent the evening vegging out and watching movies, and suddenly I was hooked – if not physically, then certainly psychologically.

I told Kelly about the Vicodin, and Kelly told Mum almost immediately. For some reason, Mum didn't seem that pissed off about it. I don't suppose she was that thrilled, but she was going through one of her more lenient phases. When she was particularly stressed out, it would be like the hammer of justice falling; but if she was more relaxed, I found that I could get away with almost anything in that drug-party world without any kind of explanation of what was going on or who I was going out with. That's not to say that she wasn't concerned, though. I had a couple of Vicodin pills on me at the time, and one of them went missing. No prizes for guessing who had got rid of it – obviously Mum had thrown it away – and I totally lost it. 'What the fuck do you think you're doing?' I blazed. 'That was mine! You had no right to take it.'

Perhaps I should have known at that stage that I wasn't the master of what I was doing.

I was fifteen, in my last year at the special school, and things were really beginning to go out of control. I started going out as often as I could to this one bar. Whenever it was open, I was there, drinking, taking Vicodins more regularly, smoking pot whenever I could. I even started taking pot to school with me. I still never really hung out with the guys at school that regularly, but one evening – it was a Friday night, I think – I was just chilling at home when I got a call from a bunch of them at half past one in the morning. 'Yeah? What is it?'

'Can you come over?'

They'd never asked me over before – I just wasn't part of that group. 'Why?'

'Can you bring some pot?'

I shrugged. 'Sure,' I told them. It was fine by me, after all, it was another bunch of people to get high with. I called a taxi, picked up some pot from the Santa Monica promenade, bought a pipe and went over just to get high with them all.

But the nanny busted us.

She told the dad of the guy whose house it was. The dad told the school. To cut a long story short, I ended up in a really huge amount of trouble. A *catastrophic* amount of trouble. This was no rap on the knuckles, no 'you're a naughty boy and we'll be very disappointed if we think you're doing this again' kind of thing. For a start, they wanted to expel me. They called my parents and my therapist in, and I had what I can only describe as a trial in front of the school administration. They were there to intimidate me, to scare me into mending my ways; and if they couldn't do that, they were there to kick me out. But I had made a career of being in trouble at school, and I knew exactly which card to play. After all, I'd been playing it every time I got into difficulty for the last few years.

I played the victim. Just as I used to charm my way out of not doing my school work by telling them how I couldn't focus, how I was a slave to my learning disability, so I pushed the same buttons in order to make sure that any punishment I received because of this latest indiscretion was much less severe. 'Maybe I have a problem,' I told them, humbly, knowing that this was the best chance I had of talking my way out of it. 'Maybe I need to go to AA.'

Deep down, I think I probably knew even then that I might have a little bit of a drink problem, a little bit of a pot problem. But there was no way I wanted to stop – I just said that so I wouldn't have to take the rap.

It was agreed that I would go to AA, so I got in touch with a friend of mine who had been a member for years.

He'd been a little twelve-year-old crackhead or some shit like that, and he was happy to take me along to a meeting. A fat lot of good that was. I took one look at the people around me, and my reaction was pretty predictable. Fuck this shit. These guys are fucking lunatics.

That was that. The dust settled, my indiscretion was put in the past, and I was on my merry old way again. Only worse this time. Much worse. I threw myself into the party lifestyle with more verve and enthusiasm than ever before, drinking to excess maybe four or five times a week.

I was constantly looking for fun. I would do *anything* to have fun, and the only way I thought I could really and legitimately be enjoying myself was if I was drunk or high. My life became one long continual search for the party. For some reason, I just *loved* to party; I thought it was the best thing ever, and I didn't want to do anything else. Whenever I went to a party and started to get drunk and a little crazy, I felt I was bursting with confidence. I became incredibly sociable, the life and soul; I could talk to anyone; I could flirt with any girl. I found liquid courage in a bottle of tequila. I found confidence in a pipe or a pill.

Sometimes those mellow Friday nights in my favourite club would become a little more wild. I spent one Halloween there with a bunch of strippers from a local club. I got completely wasted, and was fed a load of pills; when I was completely out of my head I was practically kidnapped by the strippers and we all went to the Roosevelt Hotel on Hollywood Boulevard. We carried on partying, and the party turned into some kind of crazy seance. Eventually, everything started to calm down, and I decided to catch a lift home with one of the guys who was there. Problem was, he was as drunk as I was, and despite being in the state I was, I decided it would be a good idea to bail out of the car. I told the driver to stop, then hailed a taxi. As I did so, I saw a friend of mine, who we referred to simply as Crazy Dave, walking down the road. He got hit by the car and flew twenty feet through the air. Fortunately – and astonishingly – he was OK; but when I got home our nanny Melinda freaked out at me. Word of the accident had already reached her, but had got garbled the way these things do and she thought I had been involved. Truth was, I very nearly could have been.

Despite moments like that, the more narcotics I consumed, the more fun I seemed to have. But at the end of the day, I was a fifteen-year-old, partying with a bunch of twenty-somethings. As a result, I thought I had something to prove. I could drink a *lot* of booze. I could smoke a *lot* of pot. And that's what I wanted people to see: that I wasn't just a kid. I was someone to be taken seriously on the party scene.

For some reason, I think it just reached the point where Mum kind of accepted that I simply wasn't stopping when she told me to. It was almost as if she just gave up. I think she was so fed up of yelling at me and trying to punish me and control what I was doing, that she reached the point where she just didn't have the energy. What none of us knew at the time was that there might have been a more sinister reason for her tiredness . . .

My antics were hard on our nannies too. For a while around this time we had a male nanny, a guy called Dave Moscato – or Big Dave as we called him, not without reason as he was six foot five, 250 pounds and wore a Mohawk. He used to be our driver in New York City, and one day he overheard Mum chatting in the car

about how she needed someone to look after us on
Ozzfest – clearly we were going through yet another of
our nanny crises, and she knew that without someone
good looking after us we *really* would be running amok.
Dave thought that the idea of a summer on the road
listening to music sounded pretty appealing, so he volun-
teered himself for the job. After that he came on permanently, and I thought he was the coolest nanny we ever
had – this big New York punk rocker who would drive
us to school every day in his shitty van blasting The
Misfits or Black Flag at full volume. It was more like
having a big brother looking after you than a nanny.
And he was cool about my partying, too. It wasn't like
he didn't tell my folks what I was up to, but he was
straight down the line with us. 'Look,' he'd say to me.
'I'm not telling your parents all this because I'm a dick.
I'm telling them because it's my job.' Fair enough.

Soon, though, he decided that he didn't want to be
a nanny any more, he wanted to learn the ropes of tour
management, so he asked if he could move job. Yet
again, Mum was in the situation of having to find
another nanny. And that was when Melinda came along.
The change couldn't have been more different – hip
rocker to young, motherly Australian, and I absolutely
fucking hated her. She would tell me what to do, yell at
me, dig me out for all the partying I was doing, and I just
thought, What the fuck is this?

As time went on though, my eyes started to open to
the fact that she was pretty cool. Very cool, in fact. None
of us knew what was just around the corner, but our life
was about to change beyond all recognition, and when
it did, Melinda would always be there for us. We always
knew we could rely on her and trust her opinion – in
fact, she became the voice of reason for the whole

family. And through all the stuff that was to follow, she never lost sight of the fact that she was our nanny, and she did her best to keep Kelly and me as grounded as possible. So I went from hating her to thinking that she's just the best woman on the face of the earth. And thank God we had someone like her in situ when the time came for the family life of the Osbournes to be turned well and truly on its head . . .

When the idea of allowing cameras into our house to film the daily goings-on of our family was first suggested, my reaction was pretty instantaneous: no way.

No fucking way.

My dad's reaction was identical: fuck that. And our reasons for being down on the idea were the same. I discussed it with him, and we could have been reading from the same script. '*You* get busted with drugs weekly; *I* get busted with drugs weekly. We are absolutely, one hundred per cent, categorically *not* doing this. No way.'

It wasn't just the drugs that put me off, though. I knew my family was a bit wacky, and that never really worried me; but I also knew that there was a lot of arguing at home. Aimee had just moved out and she and Kelly were at each other's throats whenever they saw each other; Dad was certainly not on his best behaviour regarding drink and drugs; and I was just embarrassed by it all. I didn't want to see all this shit up on the screen, and I was genuinely scared that it could mean the end of Dad's career.

But then, things never turn out quite as you intend them to, do they?

The idea had been a while in the making. MTV had

sent some cameras round to the house just to do a feature on my dad, and Kelly and I had showed them around. I guess we came across as being pretty natural on camera, which is something I've never had a particular problem with. In the past, I would always be the one taking the MTV camera team around the Ozzfest venues; even before then, I'd been used to appearing on TV for as long as I can remember. It's just something that's always been around, because of who my dad is, so I've never felt remotely camera shy, or self-conscious about appearing on television.

So Kelly and I showed them around, and word came back that MTV wanted to consider us as presenters for the station. Negotiations progressed to the next stage, and we found ourselves at a dinner with a bunch of the MTV bigwigs to discuss ideas. It was at that dinner that the suggestion of doing some kind of reality show – the idea that eventually morphed into *The Osbournes* – was born.

We were living in Malibu at the time. We had moved out of our place in Beverley Hills while we waited for the house that the show would eventually be filmed in to be built. Like I've said, there's no better place for partying, and that was what I was doing a lot of. There was no way I wanted to risk all that by letting a load of TV cameras expose all my antics to the whole world; and Dad was in his own place with respect to drink and drugs.

Mum sat on the fence when the idea was first mooted. She had been trying to get Dad on TV for years – she knew he was a natural in front of the camera, and of course she knew how funny he could be. And there had been all sorts of offers, but none of them were particularly cool. It was scripted stuff, mostly – cheesy sitcoms about an ageing rock star that would have been as humiliating for Dad to do as they would have been unfunny to watch. But I don't think the idea of the whole family being involved had really come on to her radar, and she knew that it was a big commitment for us all to make. 'If you want to do it,' she told us all, 'I'll do it. If you don't, I couldn't really give a shit. It's up to you lot.' I think she was aware that it was the sort of thing from which a whole load of different opportunities could spring, and was quite into the idea that if we played it right it could set up the whole family for life; but in her eyes, it was our decision.

At this point, Aimee hadn't said no yet; but she was about to move out, and was going through a really bad patch with Mum. They had just had this massive fight – blows were exchanged on both sides – and Aimee was becoming more and more reclusive. Certainly she was down on the idea, thinking that it would all just be a horrific embarrassment for everybody involved.

Which just left Kelly.

And Kelly made an absolutely huge, bona fide, twenty-four-carat stink about doing it. In fact, she went absolutely fucking nuts.

Kelly has *always* wanted to be famous. Ever since she was a kid, seeing all the attention that Dad would get, she was single-minded about it. It was always Kelly dressing up like a pop star; always Kelly singing at the party. I might have spent time with a theatre group, but it was Kelly who was the archetypal drama kid – she had gone to a school of the arts when we lived in England, studying ballet, theatre and music, and I really think she has it in her blood. Kelly was going to get her fifteen minutes of fame, no matter what, and suddenly it seemed as if everything was being handed to her on a plate. The moment the idea was suggested, she was adamant she was going to make it happen. So she went to work on Mum.

Kelly knew perfectly well that that's the way to get anything done in our family. Somehow Mum talked Dad into it – persuaded him that this wasn't going to be a nail in the coffin of his career, that he wasn't going to get arrested for drug use and end up in prison. The only way we would agree to it, she told him, was if we were in complete, total control of everything that made the final cut.

And before I knew it, it was happening.

We'd bought a new house in Doheny Road, Beverly Hills, and Mum – in her usual way – was making her mark on it, which actually meant gutting the whole thing and practically starting from scratch. A pain in the arse for us, especially as a couple of our builders did runners, but good for MTV, as it meant they could include their needs into the way the house was being rebuilt: cameras everywhere, and a special control room for them to be able to watch what was going on everywhere in the house. They started doing a bunch of pre-show interviews with us all, trying to work out who we were as people and to get a feel for us all as a family, and soon enough our house was turned into a TV studio.

October 2001 the cameras moved in, initially for a period of about three weeks. To me, it didn't seem real. I had no conception of the enormity of what was happening, and just as had always been the case, I certainly didn't feel the need to be in any way self-conscious about what I said in front of the camera. It was just some guy with a plastic box on his shoulder – I hardly seemed to realise that the stuff he was filming was going to be seen by millions of people. Truth is, that's not an easy concept to get your mind around. I was used to being reasonably well known in certain circles – my Dad's fans at Ozzfest, guys on the LA rock scene who I knew from my record-scouting job at Epic – but the idea of suddenly becoming a household name is so far from anybody's day-to-day experience that when the possibility arises of it happening, you just don't find yourself quite able to understand it.

Of course, when the cameras started rolling, we had no idea how big the whole thing was going to become. So we just got on with our lives, did what we did, without much thought for the fact that this footage was going to end up on TV. I think that's why it ended up being so natural the first time around: none of us ever really understood what was happening.

That's not to say that there weren't rules. There were, and the camera teams knew that they had to abide by them. Whenever we said 'Stop filming', they had to stop filming. No ifs, no buts, no arguments – we said the word, and they switched the cameras off. There was no way around it, and our decision on what they could film was final. There were no cameras in the bathrooms, and in theory there were not supposed to be any cameras in the bedrooms – although they were always trying to put one in mine, which I would constantly have to remove. Kelly had a camera in her little sitting-room area that adjoined her bedroom, but there were most certainly no cameras in my mum and dad's room. These stationary cameras were never to film footage for airing; they were just so that the film crews knew where we were in the house if they needed to find us.

Aside from those simple stipulations, our demands were pretty relaxed. We knew that we would have the final say on what was eventually shown, so in a sense it didn't really matter if stuff was filmed that we thought we would regret later – although that didn't stop us from asking them to switch off the cameras if there was a real argument. But when the shit really hit the fan, the camera teams were actually pretty respectful: we'd tell them they had to leave the room, and they would do so immediately. As a result, we actually got on pretty well and the family became quite friendly with them all, which was a good thing, considering how many of them there were. At all times, we had two full camera teams on site, each team consisting of about eight people – including a camera guy, a sound guy, a camera technician and a director – so there was a minimum of sixteen other people in the house at any one time. By the end of the final series, there had been literally hundreds of people working on the show, and you really have no choice but to have a good working relationship with them, otherwise it would drive you completely mad.

And sometimes it did. I was fifteen years old, remember, with hormones going through the roof and experimenting with drugs, alcohol and girls. You've got acne, your hair's a joke, you're slightly overweight – no matter how comfortable you are in front of the camera, at times there are going to be moments when you suddenly feel a sense of paranoia, and wish that all this wasn't happening. Even if I wasn't fully aware of the fact that my personal life was going to become evening entertainment for millions of people across the world, I still felt uncomfortable letting the camera crew – or even my own family – into my private life. And the thing that gave me the greatest sense of paranoia was when I had girls around.

When I was a kid, Kelly and Aimee would tease me about girls, so I suppose that subconsciously it's always been a slightly sensitive subject, something I don't like talking to the family about. So having the cameras there whenever I had girls round would kind of weird me out a bit. Sometimes it would freak the girls out too, although Los Angeles being Los Angeles – the city where everyone wants to be famous – a lot of them would come round knowing full well that the cameras would be there, and have no problem with it. Quite the opposite, in fact. One day, there was a bunch of girls over in the guest house, and we were partying pretty hard. I can't quite remember why I left – I was completely fucked up at the time – but I did, and went back to the main house for a while. When I got back, my dad had wandered over – maybe the music was a bit loud or something – followed, as always, by a couple of cameras. He arrived there to find three girls, totally naked, cavorting all over the place.

My dad was just standing there, somewhat bemused with a 'What the fuck?' grin all over his face. Now, my dad's had a pretty rock 'n' roll past, and is no stranger, I'm sure, to the naked female form. That wasn't what worried me. That wasn't what made me fling my arms in the air and totally freak out. Fact was, if this little scenario ever made the screen, I knew exactly how MTV would edit it. More to the point, however, was the fact that I didn't want my parents seeing that stuff; I didn't want them thinking about me in that way; it was embarrassing; I thought they would be disappointed with me, and I didn't want that to happen.

The three weeks that MTV were supposed to be filming us for gradually became extended. 'We're getting good stuff,' they told us. 'Can we stay for another three weeks?'

At this stage we hadn't really seen anything, so we

just shrugged and said, 'OK.' Six weeks turned into three months, then six months. The cameras kept on rolling, and to start with, I wondered if they were really shooting anything that people would consider worth watching. We were just a family living their lives – what's the interest in that? What I didn't realise before I saw the show was that *The Osbournes* would be more like a sports highlight reel – the kind of thing that you see at the end of the news. Maybe watching the whole match would be boring, but if you can just see the best bits – the goals and the dirty tackles – then it's a lot more entertaining. That's what our show was. The boring and the humdrum were edited out; the funny and the unusual were kept in.

Of course, there was stuff that I always knew would make the final cut; there were other things that I seriously didn't think people would want to see. Our arguments with our neighbours was one. Now, there must be a lot of people who might imagine that the Osbournes make pretty diabolical neighbours, but actually I don't think that's the case. I just think we're cursed: neighbours genuinely aren't meant to like us, or we're genuinely not meant to like them. I've always wanted to have that really cool thing going with my neighbours, when you can ring on the doorbell any time, see what they're up to, maybe hang out for a bit. I'd be cool with that – it's not like I want to be plagued with resentment about the people that live so close to you. But when we bought our house where the show was filmed, we pretty soon realised this wasn't going to happen. On one side was this middle-aged English guy who would stay up till five in the morning, drinking and playing music in the backyard on some huge outdoor speaker system. So you'd go over and ask him to turn it down, and he would just laugh in your face. He was completely disrespectful, and not once when we moved to the neighbourhood did he come over and welcome us.

Frankly, though, he came across as being polite and over-solicitous compared to the people on our other side. When we first arrived, they were still building their house, so we had been there for about a year by the time they moved into their monstrosity of a place. It was enormous even by our standards, with an underground sports complex complete with tennis courts and racket-ball courts in case it rained – not something that happens too often in LA – as well as an underground swimming pool and bowling alley. And on top was another tennis court, for fine days. This was no country cottage. The hole in the ground when they were building it looked like they were about to construct some kind of skyscraper, and you need big earth compactors to shift that kind of soil. All day long those things would be banging into the ground, making our house shake in its foundations and covering our cars with dust. We were cool about it; we even let their builders get on to the site through our property when they needed to – a nice, neighbourly thing to do, we thought, and one that would be reciprocated.

Think again.

These people made no kind of effort with us. You just got the impression they would rather we weren't there. We tried to welcome them to the neighbourhood, but they didn't want to know. Maybe they'd heard about us and had come to the conclusion that they didn't want anything to do with the Prince of Darkness and his evil offspring. Maybe they should have tried to get to know us a bit first.

These guys were full-on tennis fanatics, and they had

this special tannoy system so that people in the house could buzz down to people on the court and talk to them. This fucking tannoy would be going all day long; there'd be balls going back and forth. They just seemed to have no sense of other people's space. We asked them to keep it down; they ignored us.

So we started to give them a taste of their own medicine. Just for the good of their health, you understand.

To start off with, we decided to let off fireworks in our back garden. Not just a few fireworks: a *lot* of them, at all times of the day when our neighbours were at their noisiest. Then Mum took things to a different level by throwing a hammer at them over the fence. I decided to make my feelings about them obvious by playing death metal out of my bedroom window as loud as I could crank it up. The band I chose were a Swedish metal group called Meshuggah, and after that episode was aired, their album sales increased tenfold! I also carted my drum kit out into the garden and treated them to an impromptu solo in the middle of the day.

Our falling out with our neighbours was one of the things for which the show achieved the most attention; another was our so-called bad language. Strange though it may sound, Mum and Dad had always instilled in us that our language should be restrained and appropriate. It's not like our precious little ears were ever sheltered from the day-to-day cursing that was part and parcel of life in our house, but we knew never to swear at school, never to swear in the company of strangers – the usual stuff that any well-adjusted kid grows up to learn. As a result, we were actually pretty respectful with our language. But in the privacy of their own home, people speak and act in totally different ways to how they present themselves in public. I always compare it to the example of a headmaster at a school. When he's at work he's the authority figure, the guy who inspires everyone to be polite and mind their p's and q's. But I guarantee you that when that guy goes home, he kicks off his shoes, puts on *Coronation Street*, cracks open a can of beer and lights up a cigarette. He might even say the word 'fuck' every now and then. In short, the way he acts in private is different to the way he acts in public.

That's how it was with us. People, I think, never fully understood the fact that we really were just acting naturally at home. Just because we were being beamed into their living rooms, it didn't mean we couldn't say what we wanted. It didn't mean that we had to be polite. It didn't mean that we had to pretend to have some sense of false etiquette towards each other. That's not what families do – they eff and blind and just act naturally. In the end, the whole swearing thing rather got blown out of proportion; and when people meet me, I think they'd be surprised to see that I really don't swear as much as everyone thinks.

So all in all, I really didn't think at the time that the show was anything special, or anything amusing. In fact, it all seemed pretty normal to me. When the tape of the first episode started being circulated among the family, I watched it and I honestly didn't think it was particularly great. It was just my family. It was cool, kind of, but why would anyone really take an interest in it?

I was hardly prepared for the reaction it was to receive . . .

SIX

WHO WANTS TO BE A MILLIONAIRE?

Any doubts I still harboured about the wisdom or other-wise of agreeing to take part in *The Osbournes* were pretty much dispelled when they started talking money. Mum was looking after us in that respect, as she always did, and she was insistent that as we were all taking part, we would all get paid properly for our work. So when I was told I would be paid $50,000 for my trouble, I was as excited as any fifteen-year-old would be. Fifty grand. I'm stoked. I just couldn't believe my luck – it seemed to me like all the money I would ever need.

Certainly it seemed enough for me to be able to ditch those things in my life that I really didn't want to be bothered with, and no way did I want to be bothered with the humdrum boredom of going to school every day. After all, what the hell did I need to go to school for now? I had $50,000 dollars in the bank. And so, on 7 November 2001 – the day before my sixteenth birthday – I jacked it in. No one was really surprised, and I don't suppose my teachers shed a tear when I left, but I didn't care either way. I had more important things to do. Like party.

The first episode of the first series was scheduled to air on 5 March 2002, and as that date approached, a buzz started to go around. It was the first inkling we had that actually this show was going to be pretty big. But when it came to D-Day minus one, things really started to balloon. The phone started ringing constantly, we were needed for this interview or that interview. Everybody wanted a piece of us.

And then the day of the show itself. Holy shit, I remember thinking, I've never experienced anything like it. And I knew I never would. It was so dramatic, so exciting, so insane. Suddenly I was flying from Los Angeles to New York, New York to London. I was going all over the country; every time you turned on a television or opened a magazine they were talking about me and my family. There were photo-shoots every week, suddenly Barbara Walters wants an interview – a pretty big deal, Stateside. If you were to make a movie out of it, there is just no way you could portray how hectic and mad and powerful it was. And I fucking loved it.

When you become famous, I realised, you enter a special club: the celebrity club. I started hanging out with the singer and actress Mandy Moore, who was cool, laid-back – just a fun person to be around. But in the celebrity stakes she was in the minority. I soon came to learn that most celebrities are kind of arrogant, and not really the sort of people you want to be around. Although I found that they wanted me in their club, the truth was that I felt a bit different from them. The way I became famous, it was just thrust upon me. I didn't audition for a reality show, I didn't train to become an actor, I wasn't in a rock band that got signed and had a hit on MTV. I never really worked towards it, never particularly wanted this famous lifestyle – it just happened. But what you find with a lot of celebrities is that they have always wanted to be famous, and they've fought tooth and nail to get where they are. To want fame that much is a pretty arrogant place to be, so I found myself preferring to hang out with my own crowd – a bunch of surfers and skaters who were keener on partying than getting their faces in the magazines.

But that doesn't stop there being a thrill when you do meet some of these people, as I found out when Brad Pitt came up to me at an awards ceremony. It was when he was still married to Jennifer Aniston, and he walked up, shook my hand and said, 'Hi, I'm a huge fan of yours. Me and my wife love your show – we had our agents get us copies and we watch it every night.'

I didn't know what to say – this was Tyler Durden from *Fight Club*, this was David Mills from *Se7en*, an awesome actor who I look up to, telling me he's a fan of mine. It should have been the other way round. It was weird, but it was fabulous – and just part of the craziness of being in the celebrity club. Another time, I was in a nightclub and Drew Barrymore called me over. 'Come and sit with me,' she called. 'I want to talk to you. I love you guys!' These were people I'd grown up watching in movies, and all of a sudden they want *you* to know how cool they think *you* are. It was mind-blowing.

More importantly, though, I started discovering the benefits of being a celebrity in America. Anything I wanted – literally anything – I could get at the drop of a dime. I could just walk into any club in any city. In fact, I would walk down the street in Manhattan and be physically pulled into bars and clubs, where drinks would be bought for me and practically poured down my throat. I didn't have to go to school. I could stay in bed all day if I wanted, and go out partying all night. I had my own money in my own pocket, and hardly any restrictions on what I was allowed to do with my time. For a party animal, it was game on: I could buy as much alcohol as I wanted, consume as many drugs as I could swallow, all in the name of a good time.

And all of a sudden, as a result of my new-found celebrity, my popularity with girls seemed to rocket. Not that it had ever been a problem before, but it was never at the same kind of level that it now became. I've never quite known why celebrity should make you more attractive to the opposite sex – perhaps the fact that people think they know who you are reassures them that you're not going to turn into some psycho who will just beat them up – but it was certainly the case with me. All of a sudden there were a lot of women in my life, in a lot of different scenarios. I remember one day, when the show was at its height, I was partying in my room with a few friends and the doorbell rang: four girls were there who I had never laid eyes on before. They were staying at the Hyatt down the road – why didn't we join them? So my friends and I piled into their car and went back to their hotel, where it all kicked off – it really had got to the stage where girls were knocking on my door just to be with me. After a while, it reached a stage where it was not uncommon for me to hook up with two or three girls a night. There was always a woman around, and I was always up for the challenge.

And just when I thought it couldn't get any better, suddenly it did. We were told that we were being picked up for another two series. Net result: millions of dollars each. And I was sixteen years old. Pretty crazy. But I could handle it. I knew I could. I have to be smart about it, I told myself. Real smart. I had been used to having an allowance of $200 a week, so I decided I would stick to that. It was plenty of money – what did I need more than that for? But then I got myself a credit card, and I discovered the freedom of being able to take my own money out of my own bank account, so I decided to cut myself a little slack: $350 a week, not a penny more.

It didn't last long. Before I knew it, I was putting my credit card behind the bar, buying drinks for everyone and running up nightly bar tabs that weren't so far away from some people's annual incomes.

I was having a wild time, and something had started to become perfectly clear to me: I could get away with practically anything . . .

I thought I was fine. I thought I was handling it well. Fame and fortune had been handed to me on a plate, and I was dealing with it perfectly, having a fun time into the mix. I knew that people were laughing at me – it was what made the show so popular – but hey, I had a sense of humour, didn't I? I used it as a shield. I made jokes about myself. I laughed *with* the people who were laughing *at* me.

There were downsides to my new-found life. Of course there were. It's like any job, I guess. You might be a lawyer working for some big law firm and suddenly be made a partner and earn a whole load more money. It's totally cool, but there's always going to be bad stuff that comes with it: more work, more responsibility. That's how it was with me when *The Osbournes* became such a phenomenon. Where there's good, there's always bad, and in my case the good was amazing, and I'd never regret the fact that all this was happening to me. I'd get to do some cool things, get to see some amazing places, meet some phenomenal people and generally experience an amazing life; but there would be difficult aspects to it that I had to learn to deal with. I had to forfeit my anonymity, I had to be prepared to be harassed in public. We opened ourselves up to lawsuits and public scrutiny. And while, at the end of the day, the good completely outweighs the bad, the bad can be kind of tormenting.

It was quite early on when this was brought home to me. I was at a bar in LA, standing in line to get a drink, and there's this girl nearby who starts looking at me – and not in the way I might have hoped. 'I know you,' she says, with a bit of a sneer on her face.

'Yeah?' I shrugged it off – she clearly wasn't going to start paying me compliments. 'Well I don't know you.'

'You're that brat from TV.'

'What?' I was astonished that someone could be that rude, but before I had time to reply, she had smacked me hard across the side of the face.

Suddenly everyone's looking at us, and perhaps I should have walked away, done whatever I could to defuse the situation. But it's hard to think straight when you've just been hit in the face: I grabbed her arm, pushed her slightly, and told her quite clearly, 'If you ever come anywhere near me again, I'll fucking kill you.'

For some reason she seemed taken aback that I had reacted in that way.

Gradually things like that would happen more and more. You'd walk into some bar and the cool kids in the corner would start heckling and making fun. Every couple of months I'd have to change my number because the previous one had got out and I would start getting crank calls. 'Hey, Jack! You're fat! You're ugly!' And insults like that didn't just come from the crank callers. I'd only have to open the pages of some slag rag and they'd be needling me about my looks. I would do my best to laugh it off, but you can only do that so much; and when you're sixteen, you can't help but be affected by being called fat and ugly in the national press. It would bring me down; and the only way I knew how to pick myself back up again was to drink.

Even when people were not trying to be offensive, things could become kind of difficult. I'd find myself going to the mall, just like I always used to – and just like any ordinary person would expect to be able to – to find myself being mobbed. Suddenly there would be thirty people all around me, harassing me and calling my name. After a while I couldn't even sign an autograph. It's not like I minded doing it once for someone, but you do that and suddenly everyone is swarming you. It would reach the point where I would be so harassed by what was going on around me that I'd start yelling at everyone to back off. It made me feel bad. It wasn't as if I was unappreciative of the fans, because I knew full well that it's the fans that make you who you are – God knows, my mum had drilled that into us for long enough, even before the show. But I reached the stage where I couldn't face doing public signings of DVDs or books because all that attention would make me freak out. To this day, I have difficulty receiving compliments or any other kind of positive attention. It weirds me out and for some reason makes me dwell on all my basest insecurities.

And then there would be the paparazzi. Even now, I freak out when I see someone approaching me with a camera – it feels like they're stealing my soul. I think it's the rudest thing ever to take a picture of someone without asking their permission. Unfortunately, that's not the way the world thinks any more. My way of dealing with it then was the same as it is now: I do my best to look as boring, drab and uninteresting as possible. That way, even if they do manage to take a few snaps, I know that they're not very likely to be able to make a quick buck by plastering me all over the front pages. 'Jack Osbourne looks boring and ordinary' is hardly headline news for anybody. I know that now, but at the time it was just one more thing to feed my insecurity, one more thing to make me retreat further and further into my own private party.

I had the money, I had the inclination, but a party is nothing without people, and I had started to get my own crew around me. And at the centre of everything was Alex Orbison. Alex is the son of the singer Roy Orbison, and also plays drums in his own band, Whitestarr. Like most of my friends at the time, he was a whole lot older than me when I first met him – twenty-seven, I think. He also happened to be the funniest, coolest, whackiest, hippiest guy you'll ever have the pleasure to meet. A loving, caring friend who never wanted there to be a bad time. With his blond hair, and eyes that were a piercing blue despite being constantly bloodshot, he was the spitting image of Sean Penn in *Fast Times at Ridgemont High* – a cool hippy whose sole desire in life was to get high and listen to The Who or rock out to Led Zeppelin. He was the intellectual party boy. He had made a special point of learning everything there was to know about every drug: how to do it, why to do it, what it did. Alex was into all kinds of drugs – cocaine, weed, pills; later in his drug-taking career he and his cronies branched out into stuff that even I had stayed clear of, like smoking heroin and crack cocaine. Things started getting really dark for him for a time, before he got clean and stopped doing drugs. But back then, he would rationalise their use with such charming logic that you couldn't even think about arguing with him. We had drug use down to a fine science, he would argue. It was our art, something we had perfected through careful study and advanced techniques. We were good at it.

When Alex was around, you could always guarantee a good time. He lived in the Malibu Colony, a gated community right by the beach, average house price $10 million, which means the place was pretty much taken over by summer houses for the rich and famous, and as a result there was hardly ever anybody around. We could set off fireworks and never get a call from the cops; we could indulge in genuine debauchery and nobody would be any the wiser.

And there was always a laugh to be had when Alex was on the scene. There was this girl who used to hang out with us in Malibu. She was about eighteen at the time, and was dating Alex on and off. One night, the three of us passed out on a big double bed. I was on one side, the girl was in the middle and Alex was on the other side. In the middle of the night, the girl decided she was too hot stuck between two sweaty guys, so she moved to the outside of the bed. We woke up the next morning to the sound of her shouting at us: 'Oh my God, you guys are a couple of fucking fags!' Sure enough, we had both decided in our drunken sleep to seek a bit of affection from the young lady, and had ended up spending most of the night innocently spooning one another.

Along with Alex, there was José, a cool and funny guy who completed our trio. He too has stopped taking drugs these days but back then the three of us would have these crazy parties, acting out like we didn't have a care in the world. You could almost set your clock by the fact that every Friday and Saturday night there would be a party at Alex's house by the beach in Malibu. Tons of girls, tons of drugs, tons of alcohol: it was game on. We were the best of friends, and we were the worst of friends: forever putting pills in each other's drinks, drawing stupid pictures on each other's bodies when we had passed out through over-indulgence; abandoning each other when we were totally fucked out of our minds and needed someone to look after us, not leave us helpless in some bar with no idea where we were. But it was all in aid of a good time. We were *convinced* we were having a good time.

Sometimes we would party in LA clubs – it reached the stage where I found myself being banned from half of them for being drunk and disorderly. A few tequilas is one thing; standing on the tables, making a row and causing havoc is another – if I'd been in England I'd have had an ASBO slapped on me! Sometimes we would sit in a field, or take off to Malibu and sit on the roof of our car, pop a downer and get all serious with ourselves. Was it bad, what we were doing? Should we feel guilty? Should we horror of horrors – stop? And occasionally, when things had got really heavy, we would ease off for a bit; but it would never last. If we stopped drinking as much we'd start smoking pot and doing other drugs in bigger quantities; cut back on the pills and we'd start drinking more.

The main thing about hanging out with Alex and José was that even when things were bad, they were good. We'd always manage to turn it around. Stiff upper lip, here's a drink, there's a girl over there that likes you – go for it. Soon enough, whatever it was that was getting you down would be forgotten. In fact, the worse our depression, the more hardcore our partying would be to get us out of it. On a couple of occasions, we'd get blind drunk and end up crying to each other in the middle of the night. 'Dudes, we're such fuck-ups. What are we going to do about it?' Quick as the self-doubt came, it was gone: we'd banish it by drinking more and listening to Led Zeppelin. And we'd console ourselves in whatever way we could.

We're not as bad as that guy.

At least we're not shooting up.

At least no one's died.

I used to joke with my parents that we had signed a pact with the Devil. 'Shut the fuck up, Jack,' they would tell me. 'Don't say things like that.' But that's how it sometimes seemed to me. We would have these unbelievable highs, living the life of privilege and luxury; but then we would be laid low by some huge stroke of misfortune. The biggest of these happened in the summer of 2002.

Professionally everything was brilliant. The first season of *The Osbournes* had been the most massive international success – critically and commercially. Everyone loved it. The second season would be airing in a couple of months, and we were household names. Dad was on tour and it was massive; Kelly was in the recording studio; and I was having a chemically induced blast. Mum, Kelly, Aimee and I found ourselves in New York City, along with Melinda, of course, and the usual entourage of publicists, managers and camera crews. We were staying at the Trump Hotel, one of New York's most luxurious, where we had our own private apartment, and we were there to see a friend's band perform. A nice, relaxed family outing.

I had been chilling out in my room when someone called through and asked me to go and see Mum. The moment I walked in, I knew there was something wrong: she was sitting on the floor, crying; Melinda was there with tear stains down her cheeks; and everyone else was standing around with shocked looks on their faces.

Immediately, my thoughts turned to Dad. Something's happened to him. He's taken too many pills, he's in hospital having his stomach pumped. Or maybe something's wrong with the girls. Where are they? Are they OK?

It never even crossed my mind that something might be wrong with Mum. She was the rock on which the whole family was built. Always there. Always strong. Nothing could knock her down.

There was an awkward silence as everybody looked at me. They said nothing. In that instant I felt like a small child again, knowing something was going on, but unable to get anybody to tell me what it was. A little kid looking for an answer. 'What's wrong?' I asked again.

Still no reply.

I started to feel angry. The familiar rage was welling up inside me. What caused it I can't say. Maybe being left in the dark. Maybe knowing deep down, from that scene of devastation, that there was really something terribly wrong. Maybe it was fear. Whatever caused it, I felt the anger enveloping me. I walked up to one of the people in the room – I don't remember who – and I grabbed them by their clothes. 'What's happening?' I yelled at them.

And then they told me. The words were like splinters in my heart. 'Your mum has cancer.'

Suddenly it was my turn to be silent. The anger was replaced with a numbness, a cold fear that spread over my entire body. I didn't know what to say. 'Is she going to die?' I managed, finally.

'They don't know. They haven't got that far yet.'

'Jack,' Mum spoke for the first time. 'Go and get your sisters for me.'

It made sense that Mum had come to me first. We had always had that close kind of relationship, one where she would confide in me stuff that I wasn't sure if she had told my sisters. I think she told me first hoping that I would be able to hold it together enough to take over at that point. I wasn't sure I had the same faith in myself, but I knew I had to try. I left the room quietly, walked down the corridor and knocked on Kelly's door.

'What?'

'Kelly, it's Jack. You have to come with me now.'

Kelly being Kelly, she wasn't going to do something just on my say-so. 'Why?' I could hear the beginnings of a fight in her voice.

'Please, Kelly, just don't do this. Come with me now.'

'Why? What's going on?'

'Just go and talk to Mum right now. It's kind of important.'

And I told her what was wrong. Her response was as dramatic as could be expected – she rushed into Mum's room with a shriek.

Next up I had to tell Aimee. At first she acted just like Kelly. 'Why?'

'Please, Aimee. Just trust me. Go into Mum's room.'

'What's happening?'

'Mum's got cancer.'

Unlike Kelly, Aimee was very measured, very deliberate. No extreme displays of emotion – that's just not her way. 'OK,' she told me. 'I'll be right there.'

Back in Mum's room, it was hysteria. Everyone was

in tears, and nobody knew what to say. Everyone knows about cancer, and everyone assumes that it kills. And while we didn't necessarily know much about the colon cancer that Mum was suffering from, she had been told that it might have spread to her lymph nodes, and I knew that was bad. I later found out that once it had reached that stage there was a seventy-five per cent chance of death.

People react in different ways. Some people cry, some people pretend it isn't happening. My way of dealing with adversity has always been the same – make a joke out of it – and for some unknown reason that still haunts me to this day, that's just what I did.

'What kind of cancer did you say it was?'

'Colon,' someone replied.

'Well that's a real pain in the arse, isn't it?'

I didn't know what else to do or say.

We got a private jet back to Los Angeles immediately. During the flight, we did our best to comfort Mum, to hold her hand and assure her that everything was going to be OK. But the truth was, we didn't know if it would be. Dad met us at the airport, smartly dressed in a suit and tie, and we all went back home together. As a family.

Mum had the tumour removed, but a few days later she received the call she had been dreading. The cancer had spread. She would have to undergo chemotherapy.

I can't find the words to describe how terrifying it was. The cameras were still filming – Mum insisted that she didn't want to stop the show on account of her illness, mainly because she knew that it would make us even more scared if we thought she felt the need to do that. But we were terrified anyway. Dad started drinking even more heavily than usual – he was so scared that

Mum would be taken from him and that was just his way of dealing with it. I could sympathise, because he was choosing the same path as me.

When Mum checked in, I checked out. The moment we arrived back in LA, I went straight to Malibu and drowned my fears and my anxieties in a lake full of booze and a cloud of pot. I couldn't stand being at home because I knew that people – Melinda and my sisters, mostly – were keeping the truth about the seriousness of Mum's condition from me. When her condition took a turn for the worse and she had to have a major blood transfusion, I didn't even know about it. But I was dealing with it OK on my own, I told myself. I was fine. I hadn't cried once, so I had to be.

I was so lost in my own self-centredness that I couldn't even muster up the enthusiasm to visit my mum that often. And though it sickens me to admit it to myself now, the truth is that when I did get round to visiting her in hospital, the only emotion I could really feel was boredom. The conversations would reflect it. 'You doing alright?'

'Yeah, I'm OK.'

We'd sit around not saying much until I found an excuse to leave. 'OK, Mum, well I gotta go now . . .'

There was nothing more to it. More often than not, though, I didn't even show up. All those times when I should have been there, a supportive son and brother, helping my mother and my sisters through the biggest trial of her life, I was in Malibu with my friends, getting high. I would justify my behaviour to myself, of course: once in a blue moon I'd phone her up and then tell myself that at least I'd called. But I was blotting it out. I didn't want to have to deal with the horrible implications of my mum not being there for much longer. I was becoming, slowly but surely, the kind of person I'd promised myself I would never be.

When I was with Mum, all it did was remind me that she might die; when I was with my friends on Malibu beach, nothing mattered. That's what I liked so much about being with that group of people: I could switch off from my mum's illness, from the fact that my dad had locked himself in a room and was drinking himself into oblivion; I could act like all the other stuff wasn't happening. I became Party Jack – everything's fine, not a problem in the world. We all hate responsibility. We all hate the feeling that we have to turn up to something. It's why people go to Ibiza for the summer, why they head on down to Mexico to find themselves. And when I was in Malibu, I could shelve all that responsibility.

I did everything I could to cut myself off from the real world. I used to take these sleeping pills that make you hallucinate if you stay awake on them, and I used to drink on top of them. If you mix alcohol and downers, which was what I was doing all the time, it effectively accentuates the potency of the drugs. You hear about people drinking half a glass of white wine on top of a sleeping pill and it kills them. Well I was doing a hell of a lot more than that – doing whatever I could, in fact, to make sure that I couldn't feel a thing. I didn't want to face up to the feelings I was having when I was sober. I didn't want to face up to the fact that my mother might die.

Even when I wasn't in Malibu, every night was party night. At the house in LA one night, my friends Mike, Dill and PJ came over to sample some magic mushrooms I had just bought. Just as they were kicking in, I started to freak out. I suddenly became aware of the fact that nobody was with me, so I went to search for everyone else in the guest house. PJ was there, his eyes like saucers, foaming at the mouth. I walked into the bathroom where, thanks to the hallucinogens in the mushrooms, the toilet started talking to me and the bath had human feet. Lying in the empty bath, fully clothed but with the shower running, was Mike. He held a soggy cigarette in his hand that had snapped in two. 'If you don't give me a cigarette,' he mumbled incoherently, 'I'm going to kill myself.'

I started to freak out even more. I became convinced from his comment that all my friends were going to die, and I started running round shouting at everyone. 'We have to embrace life!' I urged them. 'We're all going to die, so live life to the full!'

It took me a while to calm down; when I did, I became emotional in a different kind of way. Mum was back from the hospital, and I wandered into her room: I needed to sit down and explain my feelings to her. 'I've taken mushrooms,' I told her earnestly. 'And now I love life. I just felt you had to know that.'

She looked at me like I was a fucking lunatic. She was right.

Gradually, the reality of my situation became less and less clear to me. I would pass out at parties and vomit in my sleep. I would drive drunk – even though I didn't have a licence, I would sometimes just take a friend's car and drive it round. But it never really occurred to me that I was endangering myself – I just thought it was part and parcel of having a good time. On one occasion, I went to the house of a girl who lived in the Brentwood area of LA. I arrived there with my friend Tony, and soon enough he was making out with one of the girls there. I started drinking a load of beers and doing shots of tequila, then the girl whose house it was said, 'Hey, my mum's got a load of Vicodin and Ambien upstairs.' So I persuaded her to go upstairs and give me all her mum's pills. One thing led to another, and in my Vicodin- and alcohol-induced state I ended up going swimming in the pool. I splashed around for a bit, then started floating on my back, oblivious to everything and everyone around me. Which was when I passed out.

I don't know how they got me out of the pool; I only know how lucky I am that they did. The next thing I knew was that I was lying on the sofa, soaking wet, with a bunch of friends telling me that I was fucked up even by my standards. The girl whose house it was had to go to class that morning, so she drove me home at about seven-thirty and pushed me out of the car by the gates to our house. I staggered in and my dad was up already. He took one look at the state of me and said, 'OK, Jack. What are you on?'

I listed them off. 'Beer, tequila, Vicodin, Ambien . . .'

He shook his head in disbelief. 'Holy shit,' he told me. He had no idea it had gone so far, and he stared at me, not knowing what to say.

I went upstairs and slept for fifteen hours. When I woke, he came to me and I could see the worry etched on his face. 'You'd better watch it, Jack,' he told me. But there was not much else he could say – he had gone into sixth gear himself in terms of his own drinking and drug use, the only way he knew to deal with the way Mum was, to cope with his fear that his wife might die. By his own admission, he was as fucked up as I was.

Like father like son.

SEVEN

KNOCKIN' ON HEAVEN'S DOOR

Mum's chemotherapy hit her hard, making her feel like shit. She took to her bed and just saw it through. But about four weeks into the treatment, they encountered some difficulties with the doses, and she slipped quietly into a coma. An ambulance rushed her to hospital, where she ended up in and out of consciousness for ten days, unaware of anything that was going on around her. Eventually she was deemed fit enough to go back home. Her hair fell out in great clumps. Then she had another seizure, and the more unpredictable and unpleasant her treatment became, the more I found myself unable to deal with it in any sensible, rational way.

Every day I would wake up hating the way I felt, hating who I was, hating the things I did, hating the fact that I didn't know if my mother was going to live or die. I was angry and scared; nothing in my life felt like it was right; and the only happiness I thought I could achieve was drug- or alcohol-induced, or both.

I had never really dated girls as such, never had what I would call a proper girlfriend; but about this time I started dating Kurt Cobain's half-sister. Her name was Brianne, and she was living with her sister-in-law,

Courtney Love, so that she would be able to attend
fashion school in Los Angeles. Mum had been recording
a pilot for a talk show she was hoping to present, and
Courtney was scheduled to be one of the guests. She is
well known, though, for not turning up to stuff on time,
and also for liking to be around famous people, so Mum
thought it would be a good idea if I went round to her
house and tried to chivvy her along, which I was happy
to do. It was there that I met Brianne, and over the next
few weeks I would go over to Courtney's house and just
hang out with them.

Brianne was not really into the party scene, so I
didn't tell her that someone had given me an OxyContin
pill to try. I had heard of OxyContin, of course. It's one
of the most powerful orally administered painkillers that
can be prescribed, and is usually given to people as post-
operative pain relief. But it has a pretty widespread
recreational use, too. Chemically speaking, it's just a
step away from heroin – in fact, it's often referred to as
Hillbilly Heroin – and it has a similar effect. It has a
time-release mechanism that means the effect can last for
twelve hours – like a twelve-hour morphine hit. It can
also be – and often is – fatal when taken in high doses or
mixed with alcohol.

When I was given this pill, I put it in my jacket
pocket and pretty much forgot about it. A little while
later, I had to go to New York for some reason relating
to work. I was with my friend Robert, who had been
living with us for a few months since his mother had
passed away. Predictably enough, we went out one
evening and got hammered beyond belief. It was an
especially raucous evening – I was so far gone that I fell
into the DJ booth, crashed in to the decks and ended up
getting ejected from the building because I had fucked

everything up. So we staggered back to the hotel. Alone in my room, I put my hand in my jacket pocket, and there it was: an OxyContin pill.

At first I didn't know what to do with it, but I knew a man who would: Alex Orbison. So I got straight on the phone to him. 'Hey, Alex, I've got this OxyContin. What do I do with it?'

Alex was perfectly calm. 'Look, Jack,' he told me. 'I'm not going to tell you that you *should* do this, and I'm not going to tell you that you *shouldn't*. But I am going to say that it's obvious you've been drinking – that you're really drunk – and I'm sure you realise that if this goes wrong, it could kill you.'

I thought about it for about three seconds. 'OK,' I told him. 'Let's do it.'

Alex told me that I needed to crush the pill up into a fine powder, then snort it. I did as I was told, rolled myself a line and I was away. The hit was instant, and I loved it. I did another line, and then another. I was on a roll, and pretty soon I had snorted the whole thing. And then I collapsed on the floor.

I woke up the next morning with a bloody nose. Robert came into my room, and we took one look at each other and shook our heads. 'Shit,' we told each other. 'That was pretty crazy last night.' And then we just laughed about it. Because like everything else in my life, with the exception of my mum's illness, it was just another big joke to me.

The moment I started playing around with OxyContin, it became my drug of choice. I would do it any time I could get my hands on it: with other people or by myself, drunk or sober. I became addicted to that feeling of oblivion it gave me, and I gave no thought to the dangers involved. In fact, I embraced them. The more I did it, the more I started to become engulfed in a sea of paranoia and depression. Everywhere I looked, I saw something to panic about, whether it was my mum in hospital or something much more mundane. I remember seeing my dog in my bedroom and staring at her for ages in an OxyContin-induced stupor, suddenly becoming overcome with despondency at the thought of her mortality. 'My God, Lola,' I kept muttering to her. 'You're going to die, aren't you? One day, you're actually going to die.' It would have been funny, if it hadn't been a symptom of something more serious.

The truth was, the depression that had plagued me on and off throughout my childhood was being accentuated by the way I was living my life. I pretended to everyone – including myself, I suppose – that everything was so great, but underneath it all, my dark thoughts were mutating into something more serious. It reached the stage that every night I would climb into bed and pray. Not the usual kinds of prayers that people send up to a kindly God who they have faith in and who they think will bring light to their life and ease their burden; instead I would pray with all my heart for God to take my life. Just kill me now, I would mutter into my pillow. I hated myself that much. I hated my friends. I hated the fact that my mum was going to die, and I didn't want to have to deal with it. It would be much better, I thought in my self-obsession, if it were the other way round – have *her* deal with *me* dying.

When you are wandering in that kind of depression, everything becomes about you.

I got involved with this girl. She had a boyfriend at the time, but when we started seeing a bit more of each other, she broke up with him. I was in New York again for some reason, and I decided to give her a call. In true soap-opera style, her ex-boyfriend answered the phone. It was like a blow to the stomach – yet another rejection that I wasn't in a state to deal with.

That night I started cutting myself. I didn't know why – I still don't – but I sliced up my hands with a broken bottle. I didn't do it badly enough for it to cause any serious harm, but clearly it was some kind of cry for help. But if you don't cry loud enough, nobody will hear you, and this was one knock too many for my self-confidence. I realised that if God wasn't going to take my life for me, if he wasn't going to give me a way out of the self-loathing and depression that I was feeling, I would have to do it myself. And I had the means to do it right at hand. I reached for a bottle of absinthe that I had in my hotel room, mixed it with water and chugged as much as I possibly could. It wasn't easy to keep down, and I remember half retching it back up at the same time. But eventually I knew I had drunk a pretty hefty amount, so I looked around and found several bottles of pills: Soma, Xanex and Dilaudid – a pretty potent cock-tail of prescription opiates. I helped myself to a handful and swallowed them, then I climbed into bed. I lay there, my hands bleeding and my head spinning, as I waited for death to take me.

How I survived, I don't know, but miraculously I did. Twelve hours later I woke up. I don't remember if I felt relieved or upset that I was still alive, but as I looked at the remnants of my suicide attempt around me, I suddenly felt very alone. The half-drunk bottle of absinthe and the empty bottles of pills seemed to stare back at me, daring me to try what I'd just done again. The loneliness and depression that had plagued me the night before crashed over me once again, so I called the only person I could think of calling: my therapist.

There was no small-talk. I was weeping down the phone at him. 'I think I tried to kill myself last night.'

'What do you mean, you think?' he asked me promptly.

'I don't know.' The tears overwhelmed me.

'When did you fix?'

'I just don't know.'

'OK, Jack,' he took charge of the situation. 'This is getting kind of bad. You need to promise me something.'

'What?'

'Promise me you'll stay home tonight. Don't leave your hotel room. Lock your door, turn your phone off. As long as you don't go out, I think you'll be OK.'

I didn't reply. I wasn't so sure.

'Is there someone who can come and stay with you? Someone responsible who'll see that you're alright?'

'I don't know,' I told him. 'I'll see what I can do.'

There were plenty of people in New York at the time who worked for us, but the last thing I wanted to do was call up Dave or Melinda and say, 'Hey, I just tried to kill myself. Can you come and hang out with me so that I don't try it again?' So I just phoned around to see if there was anybody who was willing just to come and be with me in the hotel room. Predictably enough, they all thought it was a pretty weird request, and they just put me off. 'I'll call you when I get off work.' 'I'm with your sister at the moment.' Everyone was too busy to come and indulge me.

So I hung up the phone, took a shower, and went out again. I started drinking. I had reached the stage where I just couldn't stop.

Throughout Mum's illness, she insisted on working, refusing point-blank to take things easy. I don't know why it was – maybe she simply needed to occupy her mind, to take her attention away from the worry and the fear that she must have been feeling. All of a sudden she was hosting this, hosting that, doing such and such an award show. She'd be in hospital on a Monday morning with IVs containing the chemotherapy drugs dripping into one arm, a mobile phone in the other and a secretary beside her taking notes. We kept telling her to slow down, to mellow out, to stop working for a bit, at least until she was over all this. 'It's only going to slow your recovery,' we'd tell her. But she didn't see it like that. I think, deep down, she thought she was going to die, and she needed to carry on to persuade herself that life was normal.

Sure enough, it ensured that she was in and out of hospital. If it wasn't on account of exhaustion, it was dehydration. She was overdoing it, and we could all see it happening. And with typical exuberance, she decided around this time to throw a party. Not just any party, mind: this was to be a renewal of hers and Dad's wedding vows that they had taken so many years ago in Hawaii. On that occasion, Dad had got blind drunk; she was hoping for something a little more glamorous this time. We tried to talk her out of it, but it was clear that this was something she really wanted. I suppose she thought she wasn't going to make it, and so she needed to know that her marriage was blessed in some way.

It was quite an event: New Year's Eve 2002, 700 guests at the Beverly Hills Hotel, the Village People performing. Outside there were stalls set up by shops such as Asprey's and Cartier where guests could win all manner of gifts. There truly was no expense spared – it was a multi-million-dollar event. I knew it would be too much for Mum to deal with, and sure enough I handled the fear in the same way I always had. As the evening wore on, a bunch of people started sneaking in that hadn't been invited – hangers-on from my crowd in Malibu, mostly. There was a raffle, for which the prize was a $70,000 diamond necklace and matching earrings. They were won by this girl who hadn't been invited by us, and she refused to give the prize back – it led to a whole drama that was just an extra bit of stress that my mum shouldn't have had to deal with. The girl in question and my mum even got into a fight when we saw her out one day after the party. But if I'm honest, I don't remember a whole lot about the event itself, because I just got wasted and took a load of pills – I don't remember what – soon after the vows were said. I seem to recall doing shots with Marilyn Manson and Justin Timberlake. I kept giving Justin a hard time because he wouldn't keep up. 'Hey,' he told me, 'mellow out.'

'Shut up, you fucking pussy. Drink!' As ever, he was a perfect gentleman, taking my ribbing in a good way and remaining the nicest, most grounded guy you could possibly meet. A pleasure to be around and a full-on mummy's boy too, so we had that in common.

Unfortunately, as the evening wore on and I grew more and more out of control and more and more offensive, it became increasingly less easy for people to forgive my behaviour. One gentleman who worked with my mum was there with his wife. At some stage in the evening I accosted them. The exact words I used are lost in the chemical fog of that night, but suffice to say that I called into question his wife's integrity as a woman, then suggested she went and got herself 'tested'. They didn't react quite so favourably as Justin Timberlake, but what did I care?

Two days later Mum was in intensive care again. The party had left her feeling weak and unwell, and she had taken too many of the anti-sickness tablets she had been prescribed, which led to a seizure.

I carried on blotting it out.

In April, after months of treatment and waiting, Mum got the all-clear. The chemotherapy was finished, the cancer seemed to be in remission, and I think for the first time she was able to look around her with a clear head and see what was happening with her family. Now that she was back on track, she realised that the time had come to clean house. It wasn't that she had been totally oblivious to my actions, of course, although I guess there was no way she could have known the full extent of them. On one occasion she had told me that the editor of the *National Enquirer* had got in touch with her and told her that they'd heard a rumour the LAPD were having me trailed in an attempt to bust me for drugs. I found out later that she had made that up, but you can't blame her for trying. But once the treatment was over, she became determined to take everything in hand.

About a week after she was given the all-clear, I was scheduled to go and film a pilot for a TV show MTV were interested in. I had gone down to Malibu and was just spending my time getting high, and I didn't even bother to turn up at my engagement. Mum called me and started yelling down the phone in a way that I hadn't heard her do for some time. 'What the hell do you think you're doing? You've got to be professional!' It was the one thing Mum had always prided herself on, the one thing she drilled into us as kids, and even more so when we started working: be polite, no matter what. The people you are going to meet going up are the same people you're going to meet going down. And if you do nothing else, just show up.

That day, I didn't show up, and it filled her with fury. 'That is not how I raised you,' she screamed.

She was right, of course. She almost always is, and I've always tried to live by that advice. On this occasion, though, just because I couldn't be bothered to show up, it burned a lot of people, cost them a load of money. It was inexcusable. But my mind was just in a whole different place at that time. I remember being in the house at Malibu, getting high and refusing to get in the car when it turned up for me because I couldn't be bothered to brush my teeth. Obviously I couldn't do a pilot without having clean teeth, so I decided just not to turn up.

That afternoon, Mum arrived in Malibu with Dave. I remember Dave just sitting there, looking at me and saying nothing. His silence spoke a great deal, though. Mum was more direct. She stormed into my room and dropped a bag full of clothes on the ground. I looked at it, then looked at her. 'Where are you going?' I asked.

'It's not me that's going somewhere,' she told me firmly. 'It's you.'

'Right,' I said, not getting her drift. 'So where am I going?'

'You're going to rehab.'

We stared at each other. 'I am not,' I spoke very slowly, 'going to rehab. No way.'

It was deadlock. I was insistent and Mum was insistent – the old situation of the unstoppable force and immovable object. I didn't know how long I could remain immovable, though, so I did the only thing I could think of doing: I ran away.

*

In April 2003, I was very far from being a svelte fellow: 200 pounds, bloated with alcohol and with a big fucking afro that was not exactly aerodynamic. But the way I took off down the Pacific Coast Highway in Malibu after Mum insisted I go to rehab, you would have thought I was out to break the four-minute mile. It must have been quite a sight. It was a Friday, around four-thirty in the afternoon, and I knew that Alex Orbison would be having band practice in his house, just like he did every day, so I sprinted the mile or so to where he lived and rang furiously on the doorbell. Alex must have been surprised to see me so out of breath. 'Jack, man. What's up?'

'It's my mum,' I panted.

'What about her?'

'She wants to send me to rehab.'

The way I said it, you'd have thought I was being sent to do fifteen years' hard labour in Siberia, but Alex took it in his stride, calmly intellectualising the situation, just as I knew he would. He was older than me, more experienced in the ways of the world. Alex would know what to do. Very slowly, he nodded his head. 'OK,' he told me. 'I know how to play this out. You're going to hang out with me for the weekend, give your mother time to cool down. We won't do anything big, we're just going to stay in Malibu, stay real mellow.'

'OK,' I said, reassured by his calmness. 'Fine.'

'But first things first,' Alex continued. 'We have to go and get sushi.'

I was confused. 'Why the hell do we have to go and get sushi?'

'Because,' Alex explained with a smile, like he was a teacher about to enlighten his stumbling pupil, 'when I was your age, and my mum wanted to send *me* to rehab,

I went and got sushi then too. So that's what we're going to do. We won't drink tonight, we'll just mellow it out – maybe sit in a hot tub, do whatever we have to do to get through the weekend.'

It seemed to make perfect sense, so off we went. We ended up in a sushi place we knew, and we promised ourselves that we wouldn't drink. My phone kept ringing, non-stop: I knew it was Mum and it was freaking me out. 'It's OK,' Alex told me. 'Just don't answer it. Put your phone on mute. You need to give her time to cool down, and if you speak to her it will only piss her off.'

But the phone kept ringing, and I grew more and more paranoid. 'She'll freak out,' I told Alex. 'She'll know where I am.' The old fear of getting caught was kicking in. So I answered it.

'Where are you, Jack?' I could hear the worry in Mum's voice.

'It's OK, Mum,' I told her. 'I'm not drinking this weekend. Nothing at all. I'll prove to you I'm not a drug addict. I'll be home when I'm ready to come.'

Mum wasn't having it. 'Jack, please come home. I'm scared . . .'

And then her voice cut out. The battery had died and I was left without any means of being contacted. I shrugged, put the phone in my pocket, and almost without thinking I flagged down a waitress. 'Can we get a couple of beers here?'

You know how it is. One beer leads to another, and before I knew it we were drinking heavily again. Alex did his best to stop me, but there's not much you can do if someone's determined to get drunk, and peer-pressuring you into it at the same time, so he ended up joining in. A few beers into the meal, we started doing sake bombs – a beer and a shot of sake downed as quickly as you can drink it. We finished the meal totally drunk, and on our way back to Alex's we got a call from José. He was at the house of a friend of ours called Eddie, and they were locked in a bathroom smoking heroin and doing all sorts of really very nasty stuff. They had decided that they really needed ice cream, so they asked us to pick some up. When a friend needs ice cream, what else can you do? Alex and I went shopping, and on the way round to Eddie's house he could tell that I was really up for partying. He tried to talk me out of it, but there was no way I was listening.

Eddie's house was in Malibu. Right on the beach, it had tennis courts, several swimming pools, a spa, a sauna, a steam room – basically a great place to party. But I wasn't interested in all that stuff when I arrived. I saw these guys much older than myself smoking heroin, and I was desperate for them to let me join in. Thank God Alex was watching over me. He was adamant that I shouldn't touch it. I did my best to persuade him. 'Come on, man. I'm being sent to rehab anyway. Just let me go crazy this one last time.'

'Look, Jack,' he told me. 'Just mellow out. Take a couple of Valium . . .'

So that's what I did, and then I started drinking again. A bit later a bunch of girls came over, and I started snorting a load of OxyContin. After that, my memory of the evening becomes a bit hazy. Somehow I ended up passing out on the floor, and I woke up the next morning feeling genuinely shit, still on the floor with a thin blanket over me. Alex had left with a girl the night before, so it was just José and Eddie left. I remember staggering up to José and saying, 'Look, man, I'm going to get out of here.' But before I did, I stole a bottle of Valium. I downed a few before I left, and by midday I was out of my mind again.

I wandered down to Cross Creek, which is a little shopping area in Malibu, and I bumped into a female friend of mine and we hung out for a while. We got lunch, and then the rest of the weekend is just a series of flashes in my memory – places I know I ended up, but have no idea how I got there. We went to have dinner at her parents' house, who were out, when things turned really ugly. She got incredibly drunk and I trashed the house, pretty much, soaking her brother's bed with beer and leaving a trail of devastation behind me that nobody should have to deal with. She had some morphine tablets, and I remember snorting lines of morphine, along with OxyContin and Valium, and drinking Jack Daniels neat out of the bottle. Once again I passed out; when I woke up again, I looked at the chaos around me and realised I had to get out of the place quickly.

My next memory is of a bunch of us heading down to the Venice area and getting a room at a hotel called Shutters on the Beach. It's a pretty luxurious place, away from the hubbub of Santa Monica but with all the rooms looking out over the sea. A peaceful kind of place – but not for long after we arrived. I think it was Saturday night by now, and the first call I made from the room was to my drug dealer. He was a cool kind of guy – he would send me Christmas gifts, probably because I was such a good customer, and was always willing to drop round with a bag of weed, any time, day or night. I bought a load of pills off him, and before we knew it, we had had several hundred dollars' worth of drugs and several hundred dollars' worth of alcohol in the room. Even my dealer was surprised by the amount of stuff there. Soon after he left us to it, he called the room.

'Hey,' he told me. 'If you need some help, if this stuff is getting kind of crazy, just call me. I'll come straight over, and everyone gets out alive.'

You know you've got a problem when your drug dealer offers you help. But even then I blocked it out.

The quantity and combination of things I did in that hotel room were just stupid, especially on top of everything else I had been taking that weekend: the pot, the Valium, the OxyContin, the Jack Daniels. When I look back at it, I just don't know what I was playing at, mixing those heavy, opiate-based painkillers with that much alcohol. It should have killed anyone; it certainly should have killed me, and I have no idea why it didn't. I think I must have just built up some incredible kind of resistance to it. Either that or I just wasn't meant to die that weekend. But my thoughts weren't trained on how lucky I was; I was simply out to get as blasted as I could. Like some kind of spoiled rock star, I trashed the hotel room, and then I passed out yet again.

When I woke, my girlfriend was still there. She was a very cool kind of person, always deliberate and precise when she spoke. She would never dream of telling anyone what to do – she just made suggestions and was very diplomatic in her demeanour. 'Jack,' she told me when I woke up. 'I'm not going to tell you what to do, but you look pretty grim. You know I'm not saying you should get treatment or go into rehab, because I don't believe in extremes, and it's not good for you to go from one extreme to another. But I really think you should consider getting healthy, finding some kind of balance in your life.'

All of a sudden her words started to make sense, but I still didn't feel I had the courage to leave all this behind.

I had a special belt buckle – it was like a hidden compartment in which I used to hide joints, pills, whatever it was that I didn't want to get found with. You could walk around all day with a load of drugs in your belt, and nobody would be any the wiser. It could hold a pretty serious amount of stuff, so I filled it up with the drugs that were still left over, then she and I took a taxi back to the Malibu house. On the car ride back to Malibu, I was racked with indecision. 'What am I going to do?' I asked myself. 'What the hell am I going to do?' Somewhere deep down, I knew I really wanted to get sober, but that's a scary prospect when drink and drugs are all you have in your life. The idea of someone saying 'You can never do this stuff again' fills you with horror.

There was nobody there at the Malibu house, so we headed up to Cross Creek again. We hung out for a while until she finally decided she had had enough. 'Look,' she said, 'I'm going to go home now and deal with my family.' It was a pretty reasonable thing to want to do – after all, we had completely trashed their house, and they were going to be fucking livid. 'Perhaps you should go home,' she told me, 'and deal with yours.'

As I watched her walk away, I knew she was right. But I procrastinated all the same. You don't just take away the most important thing in your life at the drop of a hat. So I called some other friends and went round to one of their houses. I still had a whole load of drugs with me, and I was determined that we would get through as many of them as we possibly could – a pretty hard thing to do, seeing as there was such a mountain of them. Suddenly everything went crazy again, like it had been in the hotel room, only more so. I don't really remember what happened in any detail, I only know that I went absolutely nuts: I started trashing the place, and at one point, when I saw this girl talking on the phone, I became convinced she was calling the police. In fact, she was just calling her friend, but I was in no state to listen to sense and I ended up holding a knife to her throat. It was mayhem.

As the evening went on, though, and I came down off my high, I started to feel as though the wheels were screeching to a halt. I had never hit it as hard as I had done that weekend, never pushed my body to such extremes of abuse. I was running out of juice, and I couldn't carry on. Slowly, vaguely, the realisation came upon me that I simply couldn't carry on like this. It wasn't going to work much longer.

I looked at the clock. One in the morning. I stood up from where I was sitting in a collapsed, broken heap and said to anyone who was listening, 'I'm going to go home now.'

And that's exactly what I did.

My mum was waiting for me. She wasn't angry, as I thought she might be; just happy to see me. Relieved I was all right. I sat on her bed, put my face in my hands, and started to cry.

It was a moment of pure self-awareness. I knew I was trapped. I knew I was losing everything. I knew it was killing me. I knew I had to stop feeling the way I did: I was miserable when I was high; I was miserable when I wasn't high; and I had these dark thoughts that just weren't going away. I genuinely, legitimately thought that I would be dead by the end of the summer. 'I'm done,' I told my mum through the sobs that racked my body. 'I don't ever want to feel this way again.'

She took me in her arms and held me, and promised that everything would be all right. 'We're going to do this thing,' she told me. 'We're going to do it now. And everyone's going to be OK.'

My dad was asleep at the time, but the next morning he came and saw me. He was starting to come round to the notion that he had to clean up his act. Mum was getting better; we didn't have to be so scared that she was going to die; we didn't have an excuse any more. 'I'll make a deal with you,' he told me. 'I'll go to rehab if you go to rehab.'

His face was serious, but deep down I don't think he ever believed I would say yes. But I surprised him. 'I'm going,' I told him.

With Mum and Dad's support, I made my plea for help.

And I was still only seventeen years old.

EIGHT

COLD TURKEY

Tomorrow, as they say, is another day. I woke up on the morning of Monday, 21st April 2003, packed my bags and went back to the house in Los Angeles with Mum, Dad and a whole load of mixed emotions about the pledge I had made the night before. Outwardly, I was promising my mum and dad – and myself, to an extent – that I would go through the treatment and kick the habits that were plaguing me; but when you are a slave to addiction, you don't shrug it off quite as easily as that. I'd go through with it all, I told myself quietly, now that the chemical stresses of my lost weekend had started to wear off a little, maybe for twenty-eight days. That would give my body time to recover, to have a rest. When that was through, I'd start again, but I'd be more in control of it this time. To that end, I hid a load of pot and a bunch of pills in little hiding places all over the house. Truth was that, in the cold light of day, I didn't really know the extent to which I wanted to be sober. I didn't know what would happen to me if I took away the most important thing in my life.

Apart from that, I put myself completely under Mum's jurisdiction, and she got right on the case and started making phone calls to find somewhere for me to go. There was no point in delaying, so she wanted to find somewhere that would take me as quickly as possible. In the end it transpired that nobody could take me that day: the earliest I could get in anywhere was Wednesday.

Needless to say, my emotions were pretty volatile while I was hanging around waiting. One minute I'd be relieved I was going to get this done; the next I would be overcome with anger and start yelling obscenities around the house. 'Why? Why? This is fucking stupid! Fuck that – everyone's a fucking arsehole. Why don't you all leave me alone? I'm fine, I can handle this.' When those moods descended on me, I wasn't prepared to let anybody else take control.

But come Wednesday, the time arrived for me to move to the treatment centre Mum had found in Pasadena. I travelled up there with my parents, and when we first arrived it seemed like a pretty nice little place. We walked through the grounds and in the middle of the big gardens there was a really cool old hospital built around the early 1900s. This is OK, I thought to myself. I can deal with spending a few days here. I signed in, and Mum and Dad left, then a nurse took over. We walked past the main hospital building, where I saw these weird-looking sheds – considerably less grand than the hospital itself. We carried on walking, and I noticed big fences all around. And suddenly we were standing in front of a small building with a steel door. It looked like a prison. In fact, it looked worse than a prison. The windows didn't have bars on them, because you can still break glass through metal bars; they had steel mesh plating, on both sides.

I started to feel very uneasy. 'What the hell is this place?' I muttered under my breath.

The door opened and we stepped in to a holding room. The door was locked behind us before another door was opened which led into an office. I was ushered in. Once inside, I was strip-searched and all the posses-sions I had brought with me were rifled through. All the while I was thinking to myself, I'm sure this isn't what rehab is supposed to be like. They asked me to remove my shoelaces and hand them over to them. Once they were satisfied that I wasn't carrying anything that could be harmful to me or anyone else – and, I suppose, that I wasn't trying to smuggle any drugs into the place – the door behind me was shut, and another one opened. I was escorted in.

What I saw was a long corridor, maybe forty or fifty metres in length, with little rooms all along the side of it. Each room had stark white walls and contained up to four wooden beds with plastic mattresses and plastic furniture – plus, of course, the windows had the steel mesh all over them. Everything was bolted down to the floor, and there was nothing in any of the rooms that anyone could use to harm themselves – or anybody else. A nurse took me into my room, where I saw a sign on the wall: YOUR MENTAL BILL OF RIGHTS. And that's when the penny dropped. I was in a psychiatric ward.

I hadn't realised that, because I was under eighteen, I wasn't allowed to be detoxed in a proper drug-treatment centre, so I had to go to a child psychiatric hospital. As soon as I understood where I was, I remember simply feeling terribly scared. It's frightening being in a place like that, with kids who are genuinely disturbed, know-ing that you can't get out and having no idea when they are going to release you. I climbed into bed and cried and cried until I went to sleep.

I had to share rooms with the other inmates, and was always being moved from room to room because of the constant arrival and departure of patients. At any time I could be sharing a room with between one and four other guys – boys and girls weren't allowed to share – and so I got to meet all kinds of people in that ward. It was a mental institution for the violently insane, and it housed every type of psychological disorder you could possibly imagine, and quite a few that you couldn't. There was one girl who had a problem with self-harming. Because there was nothing in the unit that she could use to slice herself up with, she literally scratched a hole in her arm with her fingers. Another girl had to be locked away practically all the time. I don't know exactly what was wrong with her, but she had obviously gone completely off the deep end. She used to write long passages from the Bible on the walls, and spent the rest of the time talking to God, screaming, yelling and throwing herself around. Another kid in there was a certified genius, but also a schizophrenic. He would come running into the dayroom where everyone would hang out – with its plastic couches and bunny rabbits painted on the walls to 'cheer us up' – then start yelling, 'My room's filling up with water! Get a bucket, now!' And he would force everyone to come and pump water out of his room – only there was nothing there, of course.

Some of the people I met were actually pretty interesting. There was this one girl who looked much more like a boy. She claimed to have been born a lesbian – who knows if that was true? – but she could write music and play piano perfectly by ear. The weird thing was that she had never been taught to do either of these things – it was just something she was born with, along with the schizophrenia that plagued her life.

I wasn't the only kid in there with drug problems. One girl had clearly suffered a lot of physical violence in her life. The drugs had affected her mental state and she used to have fist fights with all the other girls in the room, and get into arguments claiming that she wanted to get pregnant. There was another kid in there with similarly extreme anger-management issues, but I got on OK with him and we actually started hanging out a bit because, when he wasn't going off on one, he was actually quite an agreeable kind of guy. He was obsessed with Los Angeles gangs, especially the Crips and the Bloods. These are huge gangs in LA – the Crips wear blue, the Bloods wear red – and there is always a massive, and very violent, gang war going on between the two of them. This guy insisted he was a Crip, and when his mental illness started to get hold of him it was best to stay out of his way, but he was pretty funny with it, and when you're in that kind of situation you need something to smile about. The more you laugh, the easier it gets. I had been given a shirt to wear that said 'Psych Ward' on it, and to lighten my spirits with a bit of black humour, I made sure I wore it every day, buttoned up all the way to the top.

We even started gently making fun of some of the other kids in there. There was one boy who arrived who had some very serious issues. He was massively overweight, and when they walked him in for the first time, I was on the phone to somebody. They took him into a room, and a few minutes later my call was interrupted by the sound of someone moaning behind me. I turned around to see this guy standing there, completely naked, drooling all over himself. Occasionally, he would freak out and go completely crazy; we nicknamed him Zoltan, and I'm sorry to say he became a bit of a figure of fun for us, not that he really knew what was going on.

The detox started immediately, and it was horrible. It wasn't the detox from the opiates that was so bad, but the detox from alcohol that made me feel very unwell. I started feeling incredibly sick, and my body would ache and start shaking violently. I would be talking to somebody, and all of a sudden I would start to dry-heave. My body would want to vomit, and my stomach would kick into the vomiting reflex, but nothing would come out, and there was no relief. I started sweating, experiencing horrible hot and cold flushes, and generally feeling pretty desperate. To help me through the symptoms, they gave me detox medication, but you still get slightly woozy on it. It's a very weird kind of high, giving you the feeling when you take it almost as if time has stopped for a second. It's rather difficult to explain: everything seems to happen both in slow motion and also incredibly quickly at the same time. I would take it in the morning, sit there for a while watching everything happen in slow-mo, and before I knew it, it would be eight o'clock at night. I would just sit in the same place for four or five hours, able to see and experience everything going on around me, but not be fully and consciously aware of what was happening.

I spent five days on the detox medication, and five days after that waiting to be transferred somewhere else. Someone would visit me every day – often my mum, but occasionally somebody else, like a friend of mine who had been very close until I started partying too hard. He had kept his distance then, but now that I seemed to be getting things back on track, he was there for me. The paparazzi were out in force, of course, so when my mum arrived and we went out for a walk in the grounds, we could be sure they were hunting us down. They even found out the number of the public telephone on the ward and would phone it up hoping to speak to me, but they never managed it. But sure enough, pictures appeared of me walking around a psychiatric institution with Mum crying on my shoulder.

It sounds like a terrible place – it *was* a terrible place, somewhere I wouldn't want to spend another second of my life – but looking back, they did their job pretty well, especially as drug rehabilitation wasn't really what the place was all about. I started having family group sessions, where we would sit down and talk about the problems I was having, and I suppose that somewhere in my consciousness they began to consolidate the fact that something was seriously wrong. All the while I was there, though, I had the faint realisation that I was kind of bullshitting them. In my heart of hearts I knew that I didn't really want to be sober yet. I didn't want to be the way I was, but I still wanted to be able to go out, drink and have a good time. It was all part of my game plan: detox, make everybody think I was playing along, then just go back to drinking beer and smoking pot. Maybe I would hold back on the opiates a bit, but we'd have to see about that. And so I fell back on the charm that I had relied on at school to get me out of my self-inflicted difficulties: with a smile on my face, I towed the line. I followed the rules. I went through the motions. Yes, I agreed with anyone who asked me, I wanted to clean up my act. I wanted to sober up.

But privately I knew I was blagging them.

*

After ten days in the psych ward, my detox completed, the time came for me to move to an adolescent rehabilitation centre in Malibu; but getting there was an event in itself. The paparazzi were camped outside the psych ward, waiting to get more pictures of me at my lowest, like vultures circling around a rotting carcass, so my exit from the place was like a military operation. We brought our own security guards in, and they devised a decoy plan to make sure I wasn't hounded by the cameras. They drove my parents away in their car with darkly tinted windows and had someone – not me – sitting in the back. The paparazzi all thought that it was Jack leaving the centre, so they flocked after the car. In the meantime, I was bundled out the back way into a locksmith van. I hid in the back buried under a blanket until we were well away from that awful place.

The Visions Adolescent Treatment Center is nestled way up in the hills of Malibu, and is about as far removed from the psych ward as anything could be. It is like an enormous ranch – a vast, single-floor house built in the 1960s – and a really amazing place with comfortable rooms and fabulous swimming pools that were all the more inviting as it was beautifully hot outside practically every day I was there. There were only eight or nine other inmates, we were two to a room and security was minimal. Because it was so isolated there were no towering fences around like there were at the psych ward – even if you did try to escape you were twelve miles from any main street. I couldn't believe my luck. Just ten days at the previous place had institutionalised me, and the first thing I asked when I arrived there was whether I was allowed to have shoelaces. They looked at me as if I was some kind of psycho, but I could deal with that – it seemed like I was going to have the time of my life in this place.

I soon found out, of course, that it was very far from being a holiday resort, and that the downsides were considerable – the worst being the fact that it was so cut off. I wasn't allowed a mobile, and I was denied contact of any kind with the outside world. Even TV was restricted to either the news or *The Simpsons* – and only then if you had completed all your chores. The detox medication had worn off; the drugs had worn off; the alcohol had worn off. That left just me, and I hadn't been that way for a long time. I couldn't remember when I had last had to manage without some sort of stimulant, something to distract me, whether it had been drugs, alcohol, women or video games. I had none of these, and suddenly I found it incredibly scary. The family group sessions that I had started in the psych ward continued, only a little more intense this time. Then, to my horror, everyone started talking to me about God, and taking me to meetings. Now my view of God had been pretty much tainted by my time at the Christian school in LA, so when they started telling me that a huge part of being sober is having a belief in a higher power, I just flipped. It all made me so angry – the same anger that had been bubbling under the surface all my life suddenly had a focus. It all seemed so fucking stupid, so retarded. Fuck them, I thought to myself. What do they know? I just want to get out of here and drink some beer and smoke some pot.

They gave me an option. You can stay here, they told me, and work with us. Do what you're told, follow our directions, work hard, and you can be out of here in the forty-five-day minimum time period. Or you can stay here for as long as we feel we need to keep you here, and if we feel it's necessary, we can advise your parents to send you away somewhere a lot harsher. Because I wasn't yet eighteen, I couldn't make my own choices, so they could – and I think would – have persuaded my parents to have me sent away to some shithole in Utah to undergo some *hardcore* rehabilitation. I knew for a fact that some of their patients had been sent there for two years for some full-on behavioural correction.

Of course, there was no real choice.

I started trying to make friends with people. There were a few patients in there with whom I got on, people I could relate to on some level. But there were also, of course, the guys who would go out of their way not to give me any special treatment, and in doing so they don't even give you the normal treatment. But I was used to that – it had been part of my life for as long as I could remember. I just had to get my head down, get on with it, and get out of there.

You weren't allowed to get away with anything in that place: you couldn't lie, you couldn't cheat, you couldn't pull one over on anyone. We all had our chores to do – washing the dishes, sweeping the floors, making the beds, doing laundry and all sorts of other household jobs – and if you stepped out of line, there would be extra chores as a punishment. Every consequence had an action. It was just what my dad had been telling me all my life, only in microcosm. There were three levels of privilege: the better behaved you were, the higher level you were on and the more privileges you were afforded. Before you were given a privilege level, you couldn't go anywhere without one of the counsellors being right next to you. They had to know exactly where you were at all times; you weren't allowed to use the phone; and basically you could do absolutely nothing without their

express permission. Privileges were awarded if you
behaved well, and removed if you fucked up. As you
moved up the privilege scale you were allowed to do
more stuff: phone your family or a sponsor once or
twice a week; gain a door pass so you can spend a
couple of hours at the weekend with your parents, or a
day, or even a night. If you work hard enough, the
message came loud and clear, you gain trust. If you trust
us, we trust you.

I was determined to get up to level one, because once
I did that I would be allowed a pass; and as soon as I got
a pass, I was determined to bolt. I had decided that I was
in no way into the idea of being sober any more. I had
started to experience feelings I hadn't felt in a while, and
I had started to get scared. I needed something to blot it
out. And so, to get my privileges, I had to play ball.

But it was difficult. I would have one-on-one counselling sessions, and I found it almost impossible to hide
my contempt for the people who were trying to help me.
'I'm just going to ask my parents to take me home,' I
would tell them nonchalantly, the old arrogance return-
ing to my voice.

They would shrug. 'Go ahead,' they'd say. 'Ask. They
won't do it.'

Their attitude would infuriate me. 'I'm going home,'
I would shout at them. 'You guys are just retarded fucking hippies. You can go and pray and hold hands somewhere where I'm not. I'm leaving!'

Only I couldn't leave, of course, and they knew that
just as well as I did.

Once I made it into rehab, it was like everyone – my
family and friends – breathed a collective sigh of relief.
I found out who my true friends were – guys who had
been off the scene for a while on account of my

behaviour started turning up off their own back to see how I was getting on. And the family group sessions that had started in the psych ward continued – basically me, Mum, Dad and a counsellor in a room, talking things over. On some days they would be really supportive and loving; other times they would be incredibly angry when they heard what I had been up to when I was partying, furious with me for pulling the wool over their eyes. For the first session, my dad arrived early. He had kept his promise to me and was starting to get his own shit sorted out with respect to drug and alcohol abuse, so I guess he knew what I was going through. 'Is there anything you need to tell me,' he asked, 'before your mother gets here?'

And so I opened up to him. I told him everything I had been doing, everything about my final weekend before I went into detox, everything that I was feeling. We'd had conversations like this before, but not on this level, and not when we were both sober. As I recounted everything to him, I could see the look on his face turn from shock to fear. As he had also started coming off the drugs too, he was in the same position of not having anything to fall back on, and he got so scared and upset that he sat there in front of me and started to cry. Before then, I could have counted the number of times I had seen my dad in tears on one hand – and it had always been drug- or alcohol-induced. But now I could see the fear in his face, and I knew that it had all been caused by me. I didn't know what to say, and thankfully he broke the silence. 'Your mum's on her way,' he said. 'I don't think you should tell her all that stuff – let's keep it between you and me.' I looked at him gratefully.

And then Mum turned up. In the few days I had been there, even though I wasn't officially allowed to make any phone calls or have any contact with the outside world, I had managed to sneak a few messages out to her, and they had all said pretty much the same thing: 'Get me the fuck out of here!' 'They're all fucking lunatics!' 'I wanna leave!' In addition, I've no doubt that my counsellors had tipped her off that I wanted to quit rehab, and had told her to make sure that I didn't. So I guess she knew where *I* was going to be coming from during our therapy session, and the moment she walked in I could see that the barriers were up. The moment the session started, I tried to convince them to take me home, but Mum was ready for it. She flatly refused. I begged. Still she refused. Then I got angry. It did no good. It had been a long time since my parents had just said no to me, point-blank, and I didn't know how to deal with it. So I ran out of the room, yelling and crying hysterically. 'Fuck you! Fuck you all!'

Outside the room this guy called James was waiting for me. James worked at the centre, and he and I got along really well. He used to be a stand-up comedian until he had to come into rehab himself and ended up staying to help people like me. He was a funny guy, and someone I related to a lot. When I saw him, I calmed down slightly – enough, at least, to stop me from running out of the front door and into the Malibu hills. He sat me down and started talking to me. I was still hysterical, still wrapped up in my own problems, but he did a great job of making me gather my thoughts, relax and just mellow out

And then James started talking to me about some of the other kids who were in there. In his quiet, funny way he started making me open my eyes to what was happening around me, persuading me not to be so self-obsessed and involved only in my own problems. He introduced me to a guy by the name of Karey. I was just one day older than him, and although we came from different backgrounds, our stories were almost exactly the same in terms of the drugs he had been taking and what they were doing to him. I understood what he had been going through, the feelings that he had been experiencing, the self-doubt, the lack of self-worth. He was open and honest with me, telling me about his own difficulties and what he was doing to overcome them. And as I spoke to Karey, a strange realisation came over me: it wasn't impossible to do this thing. I didn't have to be scared of being sober. I didn't have to be embarrassed or shy about admitting I had a problem. If this kid could manage it, if he could battle his demons that weren't so far removed from mine, then so could I.

That night I went to bed, and for the first time I thought properly about what the people in the rehab centre had been trying to tell me. All of a sudden it didn't seem so stupid, it didn't make me angry and it didn't make me want to leave. I had assumed that taking part in the recovery process that I was being offered would turn me into some sort of freak, but this Karey guy seemed cool, so maybe I was wrong. And so, almost surprising myself, I closed my eyes and prayed. The last time I had done that, I had begged God to take my life. This time, I asked him to give it back to me again.

Our next family group session was even more intense than the previous one. This time I didn't storm out, and I didn't refuse to listen. We talked about the family, and while I would never try to shift the onus for what had happened to me over the past couple of years on to my parents, we came to an acknowledgement that every parent has a role to play in why a kid starts fucking up. Now wasn't the time to start apportioning blame, but my dad especially seemed to feel the need to make amends by telling me home truths that would help me in my renewed decision to clean up. He really started laying into me. 'You're lucky to be alive,' he told me. 'I've had so many friends who have died from doing less than what you were doing.' And I knew he was right – if anybody had seen the effects of drugs and alcohol, it was my dad. He really let me have it, refusing to hold back; I broke down and started crying in front of them. 'So what are you going to do?' he asked me.

I thought about what the people in the rehab centre had been telling me. There were guys there who had been through what I had been through and now seemed genuinely happy with their lives in a way that I couldn't remember and couldn't really imagine. It struck me that this wasn't a coincidence: they were happy because they were applying what was being suggested in that place. 'I'm going to give it my best shot,' I told him. 'I'm ready to do it. I'm ready to commit myself to this and see where it takes me.'

The moment I made that decision, it was like a chain had been lifted from around my neck.

The rehab centre was owned by a husband and wife, and the wife – Amanda – was one of the therapists who ran counselling sessions there. We got talking, and I decided to sound her out about my plans. 'I'll make a deal with you,' I told her. 'I'll commit to a year, and in that year I'll follow your directions, do what I'm told and see what happens. But if I'm still miserable after a year, I'm going to go and get high again.'

'OK,' she told me. 'If that's how you feel like approaching it, then that's how you've got to do it. I can't guar-

Brianne and Orbi . . . Party on!

José, Kim Stewart and me on a boat in Hawaii (again).

Guest presenting on MTV in 2004. Don't we all look nice?

We started filming *Adrenaline Junkie* in March 2005. Above, training in Thailand before taking on 'The Man' in a kickboxing tournament. (Fairtex)

Climbing in Verdun. (Mike Weeks/Bean Sopwith)

The final challenge of the first series was to climb El Capitan in
Yosemite. Bedding down on El Cap Spire (look at all the shit
we had to carry up). (Steve Long/Ginger Productions)

Day three on El Cap.
(Mike Weeks/Bean Sopwith)

Mike, Bean and me on the summit of El Capitan.
(Mike Weeks/Bean Sopwith)

Time for a shower. Mum and Dad were waiting at the bottom of the rock face. (Jon Turner/Ginger Productions)

This was taken at Elton's White Tie and Tiara Ball, 2005. Elton's parties are always worth getting dressed up for. (Getty Images)

Kelly and me in London at a premiere, 2006.
(Empics)

Filming for the second series, *Jack Osbourne: Adrenaline Junkie 2*, started in spring 2006. Above, setting off on the Marathon Des Sables. NEVER AGAIN. (Danny Bishop/Ginger Productions)

Sweating in the jungle in Belize. (Craig Pickles/ Ginger Productions)

A literal leap of faith. The world's highest bungee jump, South Africa.
(Michael Soppelsa/Ginger Productions)

Kill Bill . . . eat a DICK!
Practising Shin Ta Do
in Japan.(Craig
Pickles/Ginger
Productions)

antee that you'll be better in a year, but you have to give it your best shot.'

My best shot. It was all anyone could ask for. It gave me a new sense of purpose. A new sense of determination. I was going to make this thing work.

NINE

GETTING BETTER

Twelve-step recovery is a spiritual solution to a problem an individual might have with addiction of any kind. Patients who undergo the twelve-step recovery process are encouraged to put their faith in a god, but there is no pressure placed on you with regard to which god that should be. It certainly does not have to be God in the Christian sense, though it can be, if that's what you decide. It is simply a belief in a higher power, be it Moses, Jesus, Allah, the ocean or the universe. It just has to be something greater than yourself.

Before I made the decision to take my rehabilitation seriously, I had no religious belief whatsoever. The God I had prayed to at my lowest moments was not a God I believed in, and I used to have these huge arguments with friends of mine who believed in Jesus and the after-life – to me, those beliefs simply meant that they were the biggest fools in the world. It made me angry to hear them, aggressive even. There had never been any kind of religious thing going down in my house when I was growing up – my mother claimed to be half-Jewish, but only when it was cool to do so! Dad would go down with phases of mock-religion, but only when he was try-ing to get sober; his 'belief' would soon be washed away with a bottle of booze. And for myself, I had seen what religious belief did to people: it turned them into bigots and small-minded hypocrites. I wanted none of it.

But now I had made a pledge, to myself and to other people, that I was going to throw myself into the recovery process with real vigour, and if I was going to turn my life around, I had to be prepared to question everything that I had previously held to be true. I wasn't going to become an instant Christian, but I was going to have to steel myself to become comfortable with this notion of admitting the existence of a higher power than myself. I chose the natural world – the ocean, the sky, the sun, the moon, the changing cycles of the seasons – everything that I could see out there and which I knew was greater than I was. It was a big mental hurdle for me to jump, and I was in therapy for some weeks before I could even begin to put my mind in that kind of place; but the moment I did, it started to help me. It helped me to know that there was something out there, something I could pray to but over which I had no control. The fact that there was something more powerful than me – than any of us – in the world made me not feel so alone. It gave me a glimmer of hope.

Being surrounded by people who were undergoing – or had undergone – the same process made it easier to talk about these things. Even now, I only really feel comfortable discussing my beliefs with people who have undergone twelve-step recovery, because I know that if I start mouthing off to the average Joe, they'll think I'm some Bible-thumping lunatic. But that's all part of the twelve-step process: you have to surround yourself with people who understand what it is that you are going through, what it is that you are trying to achieve, people who have achieved it themselves.

The acceptance of a higher power was just one of the steps I had to take if my recovery was to be complete. In time, I would have to work my way through the remaining twelve steps. The anonymous nature of the recovery process means that I can't go into detail about what these steps were, but suffice to say that it was a daunting list. Not the sort of thing that happens overnight, and it would be wrong of me to pretend that having made the decision to work my way through these steps, I suddenly became a calmer, more balanced, less angry person. Suddenly I was having to follow a routine, stick to somebody else's rules. It was the kind of thing that I had never really had imposed upon me, and I didn't take to it very easily. I had promised to work at this thing for a year, and I really meant it, but it had to be on my own terms. When the forty-five-day minimum period in the rehab centre was up, I was adamant that I wanted to be allowed to go home, to continue my treatment by myself.

They weren't keen and I don't blame them, but my heels were well and truly dug in. I appealed to Mum and Dad, and for the first time in ages I had the impression that they could put a little bit of trust in me. The last time they had trusted me, I had abused it in every way, so I can understand why that trust had been rescinded. But now I think they could see that I meant what I said when I claimed I wanted to be sober. So with my parents' support, the rehab centre agreed to let me go, but there was no way it would be *entirely* on my own terms.

If I was going to leave, I would have to have what is known as a 'sober companion', who would be by my side for every waking hour. He would ensure that I attended twelve-step recovery meetings every week, and also that I attended an outpatients rehab therapy centre four times a week. I couldn't speak to my old friends, the guys I used to party with; I couldn't go anywhere they were going to be; I couldn't go to any bars or clubs; I couldn't have anything to do with my old life. It was like a contract, and I couldn't help feeling I was getting the raw side of the deal.

Predictably enough, I railed against it. I was much further from being rehabilitated than I thought at the time and, had my eyes been open, maybe I would have seen that in the way I reacted. 'That's fucking stupid, man. No way!' The anger burst out, and it was as if nothing had changed.

Once again, my friend James was there for me. He calmed me down and made me see something approaching good sense. He persuaded me to go with it, telling me that it was for my own good that these restrictions were being imposed, and reminding me that I had taken a pledge to work on the recovery process with everything I had for a year.

OK, I thought to myself. If that's what it's going to take to get me out of this fucking place, I'll do it.

Back on the outside, it was tough. I hadn't lost any of my fame or my money, and when the world is your oyster, the temptation to take advantage is immense. The only way I could keep to the path of sobriety was by throwing myself wholeheartedly into the twelve-step recovery process. Different people take different periods of time to work their way through the required steps: some people can do it incredibly quickly; for me it was about a year. And different people find different parts of it more taxing. For me, the most difficult step to achieve was that of hunting out the people I had harmed in the past as a result of my addictions, apologising to them and trying to make amends. When I sat down to think about it, there were a startlingly large number of people who I felt I needed to approach. And I knew that a simple sorry would not be good enough: apologies mean nothing without the offer to make things right again, so that's what I had to do. It's an ongoing process, something I am still working at to this day. As I write these words, the last apology I made was to the guy whose wife I had insulted at the party to celebrate the renewal of Mum and Dad's wedding vows. I was perfectly honest with him, telling him that at the time I was at a very different place in my life to where I am now. Like most people, he took it well and understood, I hope, that I sincerely meant what I said. Some people are less sympathetic: they refuse to take your call, refuse to meet you, and so you end up having to write them a letter. I understand their reluctance to see me, but thankfully they are in the minority.

The difficult process of rehabilitation on the outside did not happen in a vacuum. I had my meetings and my outpatients appointments to attend, but I still had to live my life, and as there was no way I could consider hanging out with my former crew, I found it invaluable to have the company of people I had made friends with in the rehab centre. Karey, whose story had been the one to set me on the right path in the first place, was one; a guy called Tom was another. Even today we are the very best of friends. Tom and I looked up to Karey a bit – he was that much further down the path to recovery, had gone through it all, and we realised that what he had done was incredibly admirable. Cool, in a sense of the word that I had never really considered before. Together we got heavily involved in a whole new community in Los Angeles that I was unaware existed: the sober community. Even though Tom lived in Santa Barbara, he would commute up to LA every weekend to stay with one or other of us, and together we embarked upon a whole new lifestyle. A lifestyle without drink or drugs.

Suddenly everything seemed different and new. I started meeting great people, and learning that you didn't have to be drunk or high to have a good time. But more importantly, I enjoyed the fact that for the first time in years I could actually start *feeling* things properly. I gradually came to understand the fact that a huge part of my problems derived from my inability to cope with certain emotions, and whenever I felt them coming along, I would deaden them with opiates or alcohol. What I hadn't realised was that in trying to block out the bad feelings, I was stopping myself from experiencing any feelings of happiness. I wasn't dealing with life on life's terms, and so I couldn't get everything out of it that I wanted to. Before I made the decision to get sober, I was genuinely mentally ill, and my perception of the world was entirely skewed; now I was being given the chance to see things for what they really were. They came in snippets, flashes of epiphany that would leave me reeling and thinking, Wow! This is life. This is what it means to be alive. This is what it's like to be sane.

And when those moments of clarity arrived, it felt so good that it would spur me on, reminding me why I was doing this and what I was going to get out of being sober. It felt fantastic.

I was lucky to have the help and support that I needed. In fact, some people might say I had a bit too much help, that I was protected from certain things in order to make sure my recovery stayed on track.

It was November 2003 and I had fallen asleep with my mum in her room in LA when we received a call from London. 'Ozzy's come off his bike, we think he's broken a few ribs.' So far, so normal – Dad was always coming off that bike, and occasionally had broken a rib. It just sounded like a repeat performance of something that had happened any number of times before. I rolled over and went back to sleep.

As the morning went on, the updates from London got progressively worse. 'He's broken his collar bone.' 'He's stopped breathing.' 'He's in a coma.' But it was weird – it was all reported to me in such a breezy fashion, and I was told so often not to worry, that he would be fine, that I didn't allow it to concern me too much. Mum flew over to be with him, and as is her way she underplayed what a serious situation Dad was in when I spoke to her. And while his crash was front-page news in all the British tabloids, in the States it was much less widely reported. So it wasn't until I travelled back to England a few weeks later that I realised how bad Dad had been. It kind of pissed me off at the time – I don't like being kept in the dark about these things, but people always seem to want to do it.

Even though I was spending more and more time with my sober friends, I couldn't help but occasionally run into the people I used to get high with. It was always kind of weird when that happened, and they dealt with my new-found sobriety in very different ways. My sobriety drove one of them literally insane. He had spent so long being so high on speed and other amphetamines that he got it into his head somehow that I had become a policeman, and so he moved away from the area in case I came round to bust him. Other guys, people such as Alex and José, were supportive in their own way, but they were still sick with their own addictions and were still going crazy and didn't quite understand why I didn't want to be doing it with them. Thank God for them, they've sobered up now themselves, and have gone from being total slobs to really commendable human beings. But at the time, I found myself being somewhat resentful of them. I needed somebody to blame my previous problems on, and because I had not yet reached the stage of my recovery where I was able to take full responsibility for my actions, I decided that the blame must rest with them. Ridding myself of that belief was just one of the little hurdles I had to cross in my journey of self-discovery.

At the end of the day, sobriety is all about the decisions you make. Being who I was and living the life that I did meant that it wasn't long before temptation was put my way; indeed, it was almost impossible to avoid when, not long after I came out of rehab, I went to see my dad on tour. Up until then I had gone out of my way to avoid being in situations where I might be inclined or persuaded to break my vow of sobriety, but in the madness of the Ozzy Osbourne travelling show, that is simply not possible. So one evening I found myself in a hotel room in Texas. It was an emotional time in many ways. Our friend Bobby, who had been working for my folks for years, had been diagnosed with cancer at around the same time as my mum. He appeared to have beaten it, but recently things had taken a turn for the worse and despite all the treatment he was going though, he lost his fight. And so I had to deal with genuine emotions with regard to Bobby's death, but without the crutch of alcohol or drugs, and I found it incredibly difficult. Sitting in this hotel room I was surrounded by twenty-four-hour party people, the dealers had just turned up, and I found myself rolling a joint. I don't remember how or why, I only remember sitting there with this joint in my hand. I gazed at it carefully. It was an inoffensive looking thing, and I knew that a few drags on it would soften the pain of Bobby's death, and perhaps make me feel a bit less uncomfortable being around these people.

Just a few drags. It couldn't do any harm, could it?

But then I closed my eyes. I knew, with a quiet certainty, that if I allowed this one chink to appear in the armour of sobriety in which I had clothed myself, the whole thing would come crashing around my feet. I knew I didn't want to be there. I knew I didn't want to feel the way I used to feel. Very gently, but with real determination, I put the joint down on the table in front of me and excused myself to the people I was with. 'You know, I'm going to go home,' I told them. 'I want to get into bed.'

I could feel their eyes on me as I left, but I didn't care. I walked back to my hotel and got into bed, unable to shake off the feeling that I had just said a final goodbye to my past.

I had clicked out of autopilot and taken control.

I had closed the book on my addictions.

And it felt good.

Sobriety, I soon learned, doesn't necessarily make you a good person. I met this guy who was much older than me and who had been sober for a long time. I came to realise that his moral code wasn't quite in the same place as mine. In LA, everyone fucks everyone – sex is a kind of crutch that people use – and he was making out with all these girls while his wife was at home. There was no way I wanted to judge him for what he was doing, but seeing the way he acted made me question things about my own life. Do I really want to be that guy, I asked myself? Do I want to be the guy who has been sober for years but is having sex with eighteen-year-old girls behind his wife's back? I knew what the answer was. But I also knew that it would be a struggle to channel my addictive personality into more worthwhile obsessions now that it wasn't being fed by drugs and alcohol. The more self-knowledge I gained as my rehabilitation progressed, the more I realised that the harmful addictions I had kicked were not the only ones I had in my life. They ranged from the mundane – I could, and still can, sit in front of a video game for eight hours straight – to the more exotic. Before I sobered up, it's safe to say that as well as drugs and booze I was pretty much addicted to sex, one woman after another for no reason other than that I could. Food was another addiction. I had been overweight for most of my teenage years, but as soon as I sobered up, my eating went into overdrive and I gained forty pounds. My diet was genuinely terrible – stodgy, high-carbohydrate food that would have piled on the weight even if I wasn't over-eating.

For several months, getting sober was the main focus in my life. It was what I did. By the time I had been at it for a year, I knew I had a real chance of continuing down that path. When the anniversary of my sobriety came round, we had a party in the house at Beverley Hills. It consisted of a meeting in the garden with my sober friends, and then a genuine celebration with about forty people, including my mum and dad, who were relieved beyond measure that this day had come.

But as the treatment became increasingly successful, and I worked my way methodically through the twelve-step recovery process, it became clear to me that I needed to start figuring out what I wanted to do with my life. There was no way I could just go back to doing the same old stuff that I had been doing before rehab, only sober this time. I needed some new challenges; I needed to know that my life had a direction. I was still only a teenager, and I needed to know that there were still exciting things left for me to achieve. I might have been sober, but deep down I was bored. Life that had been exciting before was less exciting now. *The Osbournes* had come to an end and I was living from day to day, not really participating in anything. Money was not an issue, and it would have been so easy for me to simply live off my past, bumming around on the LA social scene and just frittering my time away.

Sixteen stone, with a big old fucking head of hair and looking like an absolute lunatic, I knew I needed something to get me into shape. I had always had a fascination with the military – ever since Dad and I used to mess around with guns in the Buckinghamshire countryside – and I started thinking that I might like to join up. It would be cool, I figured, to be a part of something like that. A community. One day I even got into the car and drove to the nearest recruiting office, but I guess I wasn't thinking straight, or maybe I just needed an excuse not to go ahead with it, because it was a Sunday and everything was shut. So for a while longer I continued not having anything to wake up for.

I found myself chatting with James, the guy from rehab who had helped me out so much and who was still always there for me if I needed to talk things over. 'What

did you always want to be when you were growing up?'
he asked me.

I shrugged. 'A firefighter,' I told him. And it was true.
It was something I had always wanted to do, probably
because I was a massive pyromaniac as a kid – which, on
reflection, might not be the most appropriate qualifica-
tion.

'Well, why don't you go and do that?' he suggested.

I laughed it off to start with, but then I realised what
he was trying to say to me. I could go and be a firefighter
if I wanted; I could join the military if I wanted; I could
do anything I wanted to do. It was something Mum and
Dad had always told me as a child, something that I
took so much for granted that I didn't really ever take it
in. But I suddenly realised it was true – especially now
that I had been freed from the shackles of my addictions.
All I had to do was make the decision.

Almost serendipitously, in August 2004 an offer came
in. The concept behind the TV show *Extreme Celebrity
Detox* was to send a bunch of celebrities to various parts
of the world to have these different experiences. Some
went off to take hallucinogenic drugs in the Amazon,
some went off to a Tantric camp, and others were
offered the chance to go rock climbing in Slovenia.
Before I had got sober, I had met this girl who was into
rock climbing, and I had been totally dismissive of it.
I told her she was crazy. Stupid. Ignorant. 'You'll kill
yourself doing shit like that,' I laughed. But now it
seemed kind of appealing, the whole idea of being out in
the wilderness, having to survive in tense situations, living by your wits and your skills. It was the same sort of
appeal that the military held for me, I guess, and I
started to focus in on it. I decided I would do the show
and see where it led me – and who knows, maybe I

would be able to flirt with some celebrity while I was at it!

My boy's-own idea of self-survival was pretty much scuppered, though, when my mum got wind of my decision to pack up and go for an adventure in Slovenia. In her head, this was an obscure, dangerous, war-torn country with ethnic cleansing, bandits round every corner and a gun in every hand. She had always been pretty controlling over my career – in a good way – but now she went into overdrive, insisting that if I was to go, I would have two security guards with me all the time and a whole load of safety insurance. She did her best to persuade me not to do it, and it was a conversation that I was to relive any number of times over the next couple of years. 'It's too dangerous, Jack.'

'No it's not, Mum. It's far more dangerous having plastic surgery. More people die under anaesthesia than rock climbing.'

'It's different, Jack.'

'No it's not, Mum. Plastic surgery makes *you* feel good; this is going to make *me* feel good.'

And I knew it would.

The town in Slovenia where we were headed was called Kranjska Gora, and I was surprised to learn that it was the ski-jump capital of the world. My fellow 'celebrities' were the model Cat McQueen, the wine expert Jilly Goolden and the TV presenter Dominik Diamond. On our first day there we did a ropes course, just to get us familiar with the material, and on the second day we did a massive hike for three and a half hours up this hill. I was about as unfit as I had ever been, and by the time we reached the top I thought I was going to die right there. At the top of the mountain was a hut, which was where we were to stay and do t'ai chi and yoga – and a lot more climbing. The hut itself was tiny, really only a few metres square, with bunk beds in the corner and a tiny fireplace right in the middle – basically a dingy little shithole about as far removed from what I was used to as it could possibly be. Surprisingly enough, we all got on pretty well in that cramped environment, with the possible exception of Jilly, who could be a bit abrasive at times. She made a lot of jibes about my being overweight, which I found galling – my friends can do it all day long, as far as I'm concerned, but if I don't know you, then bottle up your comments please. I just ignored her as best I could, but when she started giving Dominik a hard time about the clothes he was wearing, he just went off on one. 'Don't be so damn rude,' he told her.

Jilly seemed surprised. She turned to me and asked, 'Well, you weren't offended when I said those things about you, were you, Jack?'

'Actually I was,' I told her, surprised that she could be quite so thick-skinned not to see that she was pissing people off. Everyone made up in the end, though, and we got on with the business of going climbing.

That first time I was presented with a rock face, I was incredibly nervous. But the minute I started climbing, I instantly fell in love with it. It seemed to me the coolest thing ever that you could just get up this rock face using nothing but your hands, your ropes and your skill. It was a high like I had never experienced. I was outdoors, I was getting dirty and I was really experiencing life. I felt like I had discovered something.

We climbed for three or four days, and although I was extremely heavy I found I had a natural aptitude for it. On the first day, we did a single pitch, or line of rope, up and down again. The next day we made our way up to a 200-foot-high pinnacle, which is a high, pointed piece of rock jutting out from the rest of the mountain. We scaled that and spent the night at the top, which was only about ten metres by five, sharp and uncomfortable. I loved every second of it: the adventure, the danger, the exercise, the fact that for once in my life I was pushing myself both mentally and physically. Scaling back down was genuinely terrifying, but I thrived on the adrenaline. Most of all, the buzz I got out of realising I could really do something was immense, and while we were on that trip I threw away the antidepressants that I had been taking to help me through my rehabilitation. More than anything, I felt a real sense of community with all the other climbers there – not so much my fellow celebs, but more the safety team of experts who were literally and metaphorically showing us the ropes. I hung out with them as much as possible, asking them questions and trying to learn whatever I could from them and take advantage of the situation I was in.

The producer was a guy called Mike Weeks, and his girlfriend, Bean, was part of the safety team. Tall, lean, strong and incredibly athletic – just about everything I wasn't, in fact – they were also really cool people, very new-age and mellow, and I spent a fair bit of time just shooting the breeze with them. They had explained to me that they were professional climbers and this was what they did – just travelling round the world climbing some of the most dangerous, and fun, rock faces out there. Mike especially seemed to have his eye on me, giving me little tips about how I could improve my technique – he seemed to sense that I had been bitten by the bug.

Alongside the climbing, we learned a lot about meditation – t'ai chi mostly – and I started to get interested in that too. I could see how it related to climbing, as it is all about focusing your energy, trying to channel it into a more heightened sense of consciousness. And as I had been becoming increasingly spiritual as a result of the twelve-step recovery, I had been looking for some type of meditation, something to practise on a daily basis, so I paid a lot of attention to what we were being taught.

One day, we were spending some time bouldering, just learning a bit of technique by a river bed, when Mike called me over. I sat down with him. 'I've had this idea for a TV show,' he told me. 'Actually, it's been brewing for a while, and I think you'd be the perfect person to do it with me.'

'OK,' I told him. You get used to people offering you stuff like that, and you never know quite what it's going to entail. But Mike was an interesting guy, so I was all ears.

'Have you ever heard of El Capitan?'

'Er, no,' I told him honestly. 'What the fuck's that?'

So he told me. It's a vertical rock formation in the Yosemite Valley, part of the Sierra Nevada mountain range of California and very popular with climbers.

'How high is it?' I asked him.

'Three thousand two hundred feet. Straight off the ground. One of the world's toughest climbs.'

I nodded. I wasn't quite sure how this related to me in any way.

'I want to take someone, train them in a year, then at the end of that year have them climb El Capitan. Along the way we'll do all sorts of other things, have lots of different kinds of adventures. And I think you could do it.'

I was gobsmacked, and didn't know what to say.

'I want to do it with you,' Mike continued, 'because I think you have a natural ability to climb, and you seem like you're having so much fun here.'

I nodded.

'And also,' he looked me directly in the eye, 'I can see that you need something like this in your life.'

'Do you really think I can do it?' Mike was incredibly knowledgeable about fitness, diet and health, and I had a lot of faith in his opinion, but the fact remained that I was overweight and unfit.

'If you can give one hundred per cent of your time, and if you really decide that you want to do it, then yes. I can put you on a workout regime and a food plan, and you'll be fine.'

I knew instantly that this was the most amazing opportunity, the thing that I had been waiting for to fill the gap in my life that had been created when I gave up partying – and I could get in shape and lose weight at the same time.

'I'm in,' I told him. 'Let's do it.'

We flew back to London, and on the plane back I knew that – aside from going into treatment – agreeing to go on that first climbing trip was the best thing I had ever done. Back in town, Mike typed up a proposal for the documentary series, and we started touting it around. Once the ball had started rolling, I went off to spend a few days in Elton John's place in France; a beautiful château up on a hill overlooking Nice. He had been a good friend of my mum and dad's for years, and is probably the most generous person I've ever met, his hospitality as flamboyant as his personality. He'll give you an extravagant gift just because he likes to see the look on your face when you receive it, and always seems to want to give back a little of the good fortune he has had. I'm so glad that my parents have a friend like him in their lives, because he asks for nothing – there are no terms and conditions to his friendship, as there are with so many other people. It's freely given and hugely appreciated. David Furnish is as much a gentleman as Elton, but when the two of them get together with my mum, they turn into these three hilarious gossipy queens – and they're the first to admit it. So a short break at Elton's house is always time well spent.

While I was there, I got a call from Mike. He was in Croatia, practising what is known as deep-water soloing. 'Come on out,' he invited me. 'Give it a go.' I had heard about deep-water soloing, of course: it's a type of rock climbing where you climb sea cliffs with no ropes or harnesses, and you rely on the fact that there is water beneath you to break your fall. Pretty scary stuff, and incredibly tough – the sort of thing that only the world's top climbers do – but after my first climbing experience I was up for anything.

Mum was totally freaked out with my new-found obsession. She had been worried enough letting me travel to the uncharted wilds of Slovenia, but when she heard what was involved with deep-water soloing she pretty much went off the scale. I was adamant I was going to do it, though. 'You can say what you want,' I told her, 'but I need to do this. And you need to let me do it. No bodyguards, no staff, no interference.' I felt strongly that, for once in my life, I needed to go and do something that was far removed from the safe cocoon of my family. Even when I was partying, there was always someone like Dave or Melinda around to report back on what I was up to, even if they didn't get the full story.

Now I needed to break away. I needed to do this thing that was completely alien to everyone else in my family, as a way of showing that I was slowly but surely becoming my own person, able to make my own decisions and to do it responsibly.

I went to Croatia completely alone, and out there I had the most amazing time. I made great friends with all these other climbers, and even though I was still well over two hundred pounds in weight, I threw myself into the deep-sea soloing like I had been doing it all my life. I found that I had so little fear of what I was doing that all the hurdles most people find they encounter when they first start climbing were already crossed. It inspired me even more: I wanted to get better and better at my new passion. And it didn't even matter that I kept falling in. It was a forty-foot drop down to the water, but it was like a millpond. In such circumstances, all you need to do is make sure you enter the water with your body as straight as it can be, otherwise you risk giving yourself an impromptu enema.

After the Croatia trip, Mike, Bean and I flew straight back to the States, where we started on the business of getting the show picked up. We were hyped up about the whole thing and ready to make it work, so before long we found ourselves pitching it to Fox and MTV. Looking back, I suppose their reaction was pretty predictable. This big-haired, overweight lump walks in and tells them with all the enthusiasm he can muster that his great plan is to travel around the world, perform all these incredible endurance activities and, at the end of it all, climb one of the most difficult rock faces in the world that stumps even very experienced climbers. I had been climbing twice, and frankly looked as if I would have difficulty getting up the stairs, let alone up El

Capitan. The response was uniform. 'Yeah, Jack. We'll think about it.' Clearly they thought it was never going to happen.

We had been aiming for a lavish production with a big budget, but when it became clear that we were going to have difficulty convincing people that I was actually up to this, we had to rethink. We stripped back the budget, decided that we were only going to take a skeleton crew, then approached some English channels and eventually got ourselves a deal with a TV production company called Ginger. It was an exciting moment – thrilling, yet daunting, because it meant that now I was committed.

The first batch of training I had to undergo would be at a kick-boxing camp in Thailand, but in order to make the budgets more realistic, it was decided that I would do this back-to-back with a show called *The Osbournes Do a Detox*. The idea was that my family would travel out to Thailand on Boxing Day 2004, film this crazy show that would involve all of us undergoing what sounded like a rather revolting colon-cleanse detox, then I would travel on my own to the kick-boxing camp, meet up with Mike and Beau and we would be on our way.

Unfortunately, events take you over sometimes. I had chosen the natural world as my higher power as part of my twelve-step recovery, and on the day we were supposed to fly out to Thailand, the whole world was given a reminder of the formidable power of the force of nature. When the Asian tsunami spread throughout the Indian Ocean, sweeping villages away and killing untold thousands of people, it was a solemn moment for everybody round the world. Our trip was cancelled, of course, but it seemed insignificant in the light of more important events in that part of the globe.

We sat tight and waited for things to recover in Thailand to an extent that would enable us to carry on with our plans. Mum was characteristically paranoid about me going over too early, because of the risk of disease in the region after the tsunami, so we waited and waited. Thankfully, I was still fired up with enthusiasm for the project, desperate to grab this second chance that had been dropped at my doorstep. To keep up the momentum, Mike, Bean and I took a road trip around the West Coast of America. We checked out a whole bunch of different climbing places, and then we travelled to the Yosemite Valley to have a look, first hand, at the monster that I was expecting to climb in just under a year. Nothing can quite prepare you for the grandeur of the place, and when you first see it your brain doesn't really take it in. I stood at the foot of the cliff face and thought to myself, Hey, it doesn't seem that big. It's a trick of the eye – with no scale to compare it to, you don't understand just how big it really is. Then Mike pointed out a tiny bit of rock jutting out into the air. From where I was standing it looked about the size of a pinhead; Mike told me that in fact it was the size of a house.

'Holy fuck,' I whispered, as the magnitude of the rock face was brought home to me. 'There's no way I'm going to manage that. No way at all.'

I had good reason to be nervous. El Capitan is about three times the height of the Empire State Building, far beyond anything I had ever approached in my limited experience of rock climbing. As I stood there and looked up at it, I couldn't help but wonder what the hell I had let myself in for.

It was a big mountain to climb. But I knew that nothing would be quite so difficult as getting sober, and I also knew that if I applied the same principles to my new obsession as I had done to cleaning up my act, there was nothing I couldn't do. Rehab had taught me, and it was a lesson well learned, that if you want something bad enough, and if you break things down into simple steps, anyone can achieve anything. It doesn't matter what background you come from, the colour of your skin, your religion; if you have belief in yourself, you can do anything. Climbing this rock face might be more physically demanding than getting sober, but mentally speaking there was nothing so hard as struggling to break out of the dark, depressing place I was at a year ago.

I walked away from El Capitan with that thought firmly embedded in my mind.

TEN

STREET-FIGHTING MAN

Before we started filming, I weighed 215 pounds, and one of the major reasons for me wanting to go through with the whole thing was my desire to lose weight. I simply wasn't happy with the way I looked. I have inherited two things from my parents: alcoholism from my father and a tendency to be overweight from my mother. I had conquered the first of these, but I knew that if I didn't put all my energy into conquering the other, I would end up constantly struggling with my weight just as my mother had done all her adult life. She had dealt with it through surgery; that was something that I knew I wanted to avoid at all costs.

I had come to realise that, especially in the circles in LA in which I moved, it's much more acceptable to be an alcoholic and a drug addict than it is to be overweight. If a drug addict walks into the room, people will smile and say, 'Ah, well, at least he's fun to go out with'. But if a fat guy walks in, they take an instant dislike to him. I was in a unique position – as one of the few overweight celebrities out there, people would be all smiles to my face, but behind my back they were judgemental about my physical appearance. I might have been getting things sorted out in my head, but you never get used to opening up the papers and having people criticise and make fun of the way you look. Moreover, I knew that people were never going to understand the seismic change I had undergone in my outlook and my character if they didn't see some sort of physical change to go with it. I felt I had a point to prove. I didn't want to be labelled 'that fat spoiled brat from TV' any longer. I wanted people to know that I wasn't a drug addict, I wasn't an alcoholic, I don't just sit there on my arse every day getting high. I'm not that person any more. So that, along with the fact that climbing El Capitan would be impossible in my current state, spurred me on to start training hard with Mike and Bean.

When I started the fitness regime Mike put together for me, I couldn't run for more than ten minutes, I was eating all the wrong things – burgers, Mexican food, all the stuff that everyone knows is unhealthy – and the weight was piling on. Mike started me off running for thirty minutes a day and put me on a special food-combining diet. This is a way of eating whereby you separate different food groups that digest in different ways, so you end up eating either protein or carbohydrates at any one meal. I could eat pretty much what I wanted, I just had to be careful when I ate it. The exercise was like a bolt from the blue; and having to think seriously about what I was eating at every meal was a real eye-opener that brought home to me how bad my diet had been previously. But I persisted with them both, and gradually the weight started to come off. I realised that my metabolism is such that I have to be constantly working out if I'm going to maintain my weight loss; miss a session, as I occasionally did, and I would pay for it next time I stepped on the scales.

Mike also started me taking green-tea pills. Green tea

is a great way of speeding up your metabolism, helping you burn off the food you are eating that bit more quickly. And he had me on a whole range of other obscure herbal supplements that he ordered from some guru of his in the deepest, darkest corners of the Amazon. I just did as I was told, and it seemed to be doing the job.

March arrived. I had started to get a little fitter; Thailand was proclaimed safe by the authorities and, more importantly, by my mum; so with a camera team in tow, we took the plane to Bangkok. About thirty-five minutes out of the city was the Fairtex Muay Thai kick-boxing camp. The camp is owned by Philip Wong, the super-rich head of a textile company who is also a fight promoter and runs the Muay Thai school where he trains champion fighters and where westerners come to get fit. The school is essentially his house, which he has had converted for the purpose. The rings are outside, covered by an old corrugated-iron roof, and all the rooms where guests stay are situated around the rings – almost as if to remind you what you're there for. The rooms are pretty basic, but not as basic as the ones that are reserved for the fighters, who live five to a room on the upstairs level. They are there all year round, and there are no female fighters, so I couldn't help feeling that there was this strange kind of homosexual tension between all these guys who lived in the same room as each other and got sweaty in the ring together on a regular basis. It was a thought I didn't allow myself to dwell on too much – especially when they start hugging you and telling you that your tattoos are as beautiful as you are!

Muay Thai itself is a form of Thai kick-boxing. It allows kicks, punches, elbows and knees: as long as that's all you use, you can do pretty much anything to knock someone out. You have to be fit and sharp to be good at it, and I was to spend a week there continuing to get myself in shape.

The regime is hardcore. You get up at six, then run for fifteen or twenty minutes to get warmed up. As the day progresses, the heat becomes increasingly unbearable, especially as you are spending your time exerting yourself physically – even early in the morning you are dripping with sweat within ten minutes of starting to jog. You go on to do five five-minute rounds in the ring with kicking pads and being taught some technique by these Thai instructors whose only words of English are 'kick', 'punch', 'elbow' and 'knee'. Strangely, their lack of English was what made the place so effective: they teach you by showing you, and their teaching techniques are not adapted or diluted for westerners in any way. Five rounds might not sound like a lot, but I have never worked so hard in my life – by the end of those sessions I would be bent double, throwing up through sheer exhaustion.

It's not until you've done all this that you eat breakfast: chicken and rice. Then you rest until three o'clock, when you get up and do it all over again before dinner: chicken and rice. And then you go to bed, and repeat the whole thing the next day.

While we were there, Philip Wong asked me if I wanted to have a fight. A real fight, not just the sparring sessions I had been practising. I didn't quite know what to say, but he was persistent. He could train me up, he promised, and in a month I would be ready to fight somebody for real. I shook my head. 'I can't fight,' I told him. 'I'm not a fighter, it's not what I'm about. I'm only here to get fit.'

Philip disagreed. 'You'll be fine,' he assured me. 'We'll train you hard enough, and I can see that you have the courage to do it.'

In the end I agreed, more to be polite than anything else, though I think I must have sounded more keen than I actually was. 'OK,' I said. 'Fuck it. What's the worst that can happen? I get knocked out. Let's give it a go.'

We spent an initial week at the training camp, then we travelled to a detox place for a week-long colon cleanse, which was just as intense as it sounds. We were booked in to a place called The Sanctuary on an island called Ko Panyang – supposedly the inspiration for Alex Garland's novel *The Beach*. It was a cool place, full of hippies, and I remember thinking that if I was still partying I would've moved there: the perfect place for cheap alcohol and all the drugs you could ever want. It was ironic that in the middle of all that was this amazing detox centre – the local wisdom was that you would go out there and detox just to retox. But for us, partying was most certainly not on the agenda. For seven days you are not allowed to eat a thing, except fibre shakes and special supplements to stop your body from going into shock; and you undergo a colonic irrigation twice a day. For someone who likes their food as much as me, it was a genuinely horrible experience. Day after day of unparalleled boredom, punctuated only by the opportunity to shove a tube up your arse and have four litres of liquid pumped in and out.

The idea is that, as we eat things as part of our modern diet that we're not really supposed to, toxins build up in our gut that shouldn't be there. The colon cleanse is a way of getting rid of these toxins. A straightforward idea in principle; and in practice it's pretty easy too. You go into a little booth where there is a wooden plank for you to lie on. In the middle of the plank is a hole with a plastic tube sticking out of it. You shimmy down the tube, lie on your back and let the fun begin. You are told to try and hold the water in for as long as you can, because that way it goes further up your intestinal tract; but it can be uncomfortable as the pressure builds up, and in any case the first time you do it you have no hope of holding on for more than a few seconds. I won't go into the grisly details of what happens once the enema starts – suffice to say it's pretty disgusting – but I will admit that once it finished I felt good on it. The place where we went specialised in coffee enemas – two cups of coffee mixed in with the water on the basis that coffee is a natural laxative – and once it had done its job I felt as light as a feather, although that may have had more to do with the fact that I hadn't eaten for seven days. The hunger drove me to distraction – I started to dream about piles of scrambled egg on toast, and I couldn't wait for it to be over.

Once it was, and we had rewarded ourselves by going and eating at the local restaurant that was reputed to be the best for miles around, it was back to Fairtex for more Muay Thai training. I was half hoping that the crackpot idea of me having this professional fight would have been forgotten about in the intervening few days, but that was wishful thinking. I was hurled straight back into the training regime, which was even more intense than before as I tried to get myself match fit. The weight started to fall off fast, and I learned a few more moves in the ring. But all the while the build-up to this fight was increasing and increasing, and it started to get to me. I just didn't feel ready. After all, I had only been kick-boxing for a couple of weeks: what chance could I possibly have against a seasoned professional?

As the days went by I started to get scared and worried. What had I got myself into? I was going to have the living shit kicked out of me. But there was no real turning back: I had made my promise to have the fight, and the wheels were in motion. And a small part of me still wanted to do it, I suppose. Even if I lost, which I probably would do, it would be a good story at the end of the day – provided I still had all my faculties in order to recount it.

As the fight day approached, I started to learn a little bit about my opponent. He went by the moniker of The Man, and in his day he was a feared opponent. He had been retired for a while now, and this was his comeback fight. He had a weak punch, I was told, but a strong kick; more importantly he had years of fighting experience under his belt. He had been in the ring countless times; I had never had a single professional fight. To put it bluntly, I was shit scared.

The fight was to be held in Pattaya, about two and a half hours from the training school and a very seedy place indeed – the kind of town you expect to be full of sex tourists. We arrived there a few hours before the fight, and I realised that the whole thing was turning into something I really didn't want it to be. Slowly but surely over the past few weeks the press had got wind of the story that I was going to have this fight, and sure enough the paparazzi were out in force to document it. The last thing I needed to worry about was the press – I had more important things to take care of, like the fact that I was about to get an arse-beating – so I tried to put all that stuff from my mind. The hours until the fight were ticking away, and with each moment that passed that feeling of fear in my stomach grew a little bit stronger.

Mum and Dad had agreed to fly out for the fight; when they arrived I could see the worry etched on their faces. What the hell was their little boy up to now? I did my best to appear nonchalant about it in front of them, my way of trying to spare them a bit of the anxiety they were feeling. I tried to explain to them that the fight was not a foregone conclusion. I had certain things on my side. One was that my trainer, Happiday, was the most legendary Muay Thai fighter ever – his nickname was The Axe because he broke so many legs with his kicks. They have statues of him all around Thailand – he's the Muhammad Ali of Muay Thai – and it was encouraging to have him as my trainer. Not encouraging enough for me to think that I wasn't going to have the crap kicked out of me, though.

The night of the fight arrived. There were to be a number of fights on that evening, and I was about eighth in line. I sneaked into the audience to watch the proceedings, not knowing whether I would find it encouraging or not. It was scorching hot, and the audience themselves were going wild, waving money in the air and screaming on their champions as they made mincemeat of each other in the ring. I saw Mum and Dad in amongst it all, jet-lagged, surrounded by sweat and mosquitoes, and bemused by this weird situation in which they found themselves. For me, it was horrific to watch: these guys were giving and receiving vicious punches and kicks, and most of the fights were being won by knock-outs. That was what I could expect. There was no play-fighting here.

Sooner than I expected, I was watching the fight before mine. Sure enough, the loser was knocked out.

But as I watched it happen, a strange sense of calm descended on me. 'Ten minutes, Jack,' I heard someone say. They were words that I had been dreading all evening, but now my time had come I felt totally relaxed and focused. The Muay Thai way is that you don't warm up before a fight because you need to save all the energy you have for the actual combat. Instead, they rub a special oil all over your body that warms and loosens all your muscles. They applied it to my skin and I felt the peculiar sensation of heat all over me. Then they rubbed Vaseline over my face so that the punches I was about to receive would slide off. And then I was led into the ring.

The tradition is that before the fight starts, the contenders perform a ceremonial dance called the *Wai Kru*. It consists of three bows; on the third bow you focus on something dear to you as a way of showing respect towards the sacredness of the fight that is about to begin. We performed the *Wai Kru* to the cheers of the audience, stepped back into our corners, and the bell rang. The fight was on.

I had a plan. Mike had told me that the Thai fighters tend to take it pretty easy in the first round, so the best way to deal with them is unload everything you've got right at the beginning when they're least expecting it. The theory was good, but I didn't know if I was adept enough to pull it off. I was going to give it my best shot, though. As soon as it began, I forgot my fear. But that didn't mean I was impervious to the pain The Man inflicted on me as he delivered a crushing kick to my leg. I felt it shriek through me, but I knew I couldn't let it put me down, so through sheer force of will I carried on. I threw my best punches and kicks at him, with all the vigour I could muster, and he did seem to be taken aback by the viciousness of my assault. It didn't stop him from whacking me in the face, though, and at one point he launched a kick that pretty much lifted me off the ground. All in all, though, I was pleased with my performance. If I went down after that, at least I would have a bit of dignity intact. Before I knew it the first round was over.

I didn't feel too exhausted after the first round. In practice sessions, you fight five-minute rounds with a one-minute rest, but in a fight situation you have three-minute rounds with two-minute rests. So although I was battered and bruised, I was still in pretty good shape. Happiday was in my corner – a good-luck charm if ever there was one, and the respect he engendered in everyone there was awesome. He wiped me down, told me I was doing fine and before I knew it the second round had begun.

It was over so quickly. I manoeuvred him into a corner, then blasted him with a flurry of punches and kicks. He started to go down, and as he did so I kicked him hard in the head. And that was it. A knock-out.

I had done it.

The audience went wild. I looked out of the ring and saw my parents sitting there. The look on my dad's face in particular was something to cherish – shock, excitement and real elation all in one. I don't think they could believe what I had just achieved any more than I could. Mike hugged me. Mum and Dad hugged me. We all had tears in our eyes.

We all knew that I had jumped another hurdle.

Mum and Dad were staying at the Peninsula Hotel in Bangkok, so I went back with them and enjoyed the well-earned luxuries of a hot bath and room service. I had come a long way since my arrival at the Muay Thai camp, but the truth was that I wouldn't be sorry to see the back of the place – it had been hard, hot, uncomfortable work and I was ready for a change of scene. So when my parents returned to LA, Mike, Bean and I headed down to Krabi in the south of the country, which is a well-known climbing region. We spent two weeks there, climbing every day and really laying the groundwork for the task we had ahead.

It was while we were in Krabi, though, that the first feelings of genuine fear set in. Climbing El Capitan was going to be a monumental feat. The faces we were attempting were more difficult, and higher up, than anything I had attempted before, and I started to realise that despite my experiences at the Muay Thai camp, I wasn't nearly fit enough to manage El Cap. Moreover, I started to develop a fear of heights – not vertigo, exactly, but a worry that my lack of fitness was going to let me down and I would end up hurting myself badly. It was something I was going to have to conquer if this thing was going to go any further. Climbing in Thailand was especially difficult because it's so hot. Your sweaty palms end up slipping on the rock, and the more chalk you use, the more it turns to toothpaste in your hands. All this compounded my insecurities in my ability. It was a sobering couple of weeks.

Mike and Bean went back to London; I returned to LA for a week, where I caught up on my sleep and had loads of people look at me like they didn't really recognise me. I'd walk up to a club and the bouncers, who I knew, would put their hands up to deny me entry. 'It's Jack,' I'd tell them, and they would be genuinely astonished at how different I looked. The punishing regime I had put myself through had clearly had some beneficial effects on my figure. Mike had bet me that I would put on weight during my time in LA; I took up the gauntlet, and promised him that if I didn't manage to lose five pounds, I would take him to Elton John's White Tie and Tiara ball. In the end, I actually shed ten pounds in that one week.

I wasn't allowed too much R & R, though, because when my break was over Mike, Bean and I found ourselves at the Gorges du Verdon in the South of France. It's a thousand-foot canyon, spectacularly beautiful, and a magnet for climbers. I was to spend time here taking my climbing skills to a whole other level. The most important thing that Mike and Bean wanted to teach me was to trust the rope. We were to practise a type of ascent called sport leading. As you climb, you put karabiners called Quickdraws into bolts in the wall, then you clip the rope into the karabiner. That way, if you fall, you only end up falling twice the distance between you and the last bolt you've put in the rock face – generally about ten or twelve feet. It sounds straightforward in theory, and perhaps doesn't seem like a great distance, but to learn how to fall safely and without fear is a demanding process. You have to battle with any demons you have about how high up you are, and learn to trust the rope. I had had a couple of meltdowns with regard to my vague fear of heights, and now was the time to work on exorcising that fear. The first time I took a fall on purpose, I was a thousand feet up. It took me ages to summon up the courage to do it – your every instinct is to stop yourself from falling, and to let go requires a strength of will that I knew I had inside me but which I found difficult to tap into. My body started shaking; I was crying in desperation at what I had to do.

But in the end I managed it. Another box ticked; another hurdle crossed.

From Verdon, we travelled to Chamonix in the French Alps to practise ice climbing. The idea was to climb this huge ice face with me leading the entire way, and I was freaking out about the whole idea. We spent a bit of time practising on some smaller faces, so I could learn how to use crampons and ice picks, but the idea of being in charge of a full ascent up something much bigger was a difficult one to deal with. In order to climb up ice, you twist these enormous screws into the ice at an upward angle. What you have to remember, though, is that ice is water. Water moves. If there is any kind of temperature fluctuation, it can be a very risky process indeed, and this was the height of summer.

The day of the ascent arrived. We packed our back-packs, which must have weighed the best part of fifty pounds, and we set off on a seven-mile uphill hike to this mountain hut that we would use as a base camp. It takes most people five or six hours; it took me nine. The trek starts off at pretty much a forty-five degree angle, and then you have to start crossing these ice patches – basically big sheets of ice with snow on top. You put your crampons on, but if you slip, you end up sliding pretty much half the way back home, which is a scary prospect. And you would be walking though snow when you would suddenly find that you were in it up to your hips and struggling to climb out. I wasn't too far into the trek before I was completely fucked, and it really brought home to me how out of shape I was despite all the training I had been doing. Mike and Bean were unsympathetic. Correction: they were absolute bastards. They were miles ahead of me, and every time they looked back they started making fun, mooning me, shouting derision. Thanks, guys. It was physically just about the toughest thing I had had to do, and I wanted to cry all the way.

By the time I made it up there, I felt physically sick, my throat was swollen up and I had a fever. I hadn't eaten all day and I was utterly exhausted. There were rumours of a snow storm the following day, but I was too tired to pay any attention to that – if the ice climb proper was going to be anything like I had just experienced, I wasn't too hyped about doing it anyway. I ate and went straight to bed; but you don't sleep well at altitude, and I ended up sleeping-in the following morning, which meant we didn't leave for that day's climbing until much later than we anticipated.

We hiked to the base of the ice climb, but by the time we arrived the weather had taken a severe turn for the worse. There was no way we could attempt it. 'OK,' I said, slightly relieved that I had been given a reprieve. 'What do we do now?' Surely we weren't going to have to hike all the way back to the hut in order to hike all the way back again when the weather cleared.

'We dig a snow cave,' Mike told us. 'See what the weather brings tomorrow.'

It took a good few hours to build the snow cave. You take a prodder, an implement that you use for trying to find people in an avalanche, and prod around for the deepest patch of snow you can find. Then you dig two holes which meet in the middle, and there's your cave. It doesn't sound very practical, but the idea is that, as ice is always the same temperature – zero degrees Celsius – it doesn't matter how cold it gets outside. It could be minus twenty, but in your snow cave it will still be a more tolerable zero degrees. If the snow cave is not built correctly, there is a risk of the roof collapsing, but fortunately I was with professionals. Had somebody come along and started jumping on the roof, we might have been in trouble; but in fact we were pretty safe, and when the storm came along, we were glad of our exertions.

Things can be counter-intuitive once you are inside. You would assume, for example, that in those sort of temperatures, the more you wear the better. I found, as I was lying in that cramped little cave, that I warmed up when I shed some of the layers I was wearing. Logistics can be difficult in there too. In the middle of the night, the storm started truly howling around us. It was like the end of the world – thunder, lightning, snow, hail. Even if it had not been so terrible outside, the three slumbering bodies between me and the exit, and the fact that the ceiling was only two and a half feet above me, would have stopped me from venturing outside. Typically, though, I became overwhelmed with a need to take a piss. It's amazing how useful an empty bottle can be when you're half way up a mountain . . .

The next morning we took stock. The weather was clearly still volatile: we couldn't rely on its consistency if we were to try the ascent, and we would have put our lives at risk. So we took the sensible course of action, turned around and headed back down. For me it was a huge fucking relief. We may not have done the big climb, but I still had ice burns on my hands and my face was peeling from sun exposure.

Mike, Bean and I drove back to London and the very next day I attended an awards ceremony. I hadn't been seen in the press for some time by this stage, and when I arrived I encountered the same problem I had had in LA. 'Who are you?'

'Jack Osbourne.'

The look on their faces was a picture. As I walked up the red carpet, I was aware that there were no camera flashes. Normally at an event like that you can't see for flashbulbs, but the paparazzi obviously had no idea who I was, I looked so different. Then, from the crowd, I heard someone shout, 'It's Jack!' Instantly it was bedlam: a blinding sea of camera flashes, people calling out at me wanting to get a picture of the new look.

And you know what? It felt great. At the party I received a lot of compliments about the way I was looking, including some encouraging words from Kelly Holmes the runner, which made me feel very good about myself indeed. She even gave me a shout-out from the stage when she won her award.

I hadn't gone out of my way to look for that kind of reaction; but when I received it, it spurred me on to complete what I had set out to do.

While I was doing all this, back in LA Kelly was struggling. She didn't have the same difficulties with drink and drugs as I did, but she had been in and out of treatment for a while now, realising that whatever it was she was into had become her master. She would check herself in, then come out again only to get drunk once more.

In the meantime, Mike, Bean and I had headed back to France for more training. Céüse, near the city of Gap, is a near-legendary climbing region, and we had packed a whole bunch of climbing and camping gear into a tiny two-door Audi and sped down there to get some more practice in. While I was there Kelly got bad again: bridges were being burned, relationships were being ruined, and I got a tearful call from Mum. 'I don't know what to do, Jack,' she cried.

So I spoke to Kelly. 'What are you going to do about this?' I asked her.

'I don't' know.' I could hear the desperation in her voice.

'Why don't you come out to France, spend some time with us? We can sit and talk these things through. I've been there, so maybe I can help.'

I wasn't sure if she would take me up on my offer – it wasn't really her scene, to put it mildly – but I thought it would be good for her to be put in a position where she would be doing something physically active every single day. Surprisingly enough, she agreed. And to a certain extent she threw herself into the lifestyle, camping with us and doing as much climbing as she was able. Of course, Jack and Kelly being Jack and Kelly, we got on each other's nerves a bit, but that was to be expected. I think Kelly was frustrated by the fact that I didn't care how far outside her comfort zone she was, living in a tent, using communal showers, eating basic food. I knew this was the craziest thing she had ever done, but I refused to react to her tears and her tantrums. 'Stop crying! Keep hiking! You're too slow!' The Mike and Bean way of doing things must have rubbed off on me. OK, I was acting like a dick, but Kelly seemed to respond to it and started doing really well.

For myself, things really started to click into place in Céüse. My climbing skills improved immeasurably, and the weight continued to drop off me – I was actually beginning to get kind of skinny. I was climbing more efficiently, leading more – and harder – routes, and I was also given the opportunity to try my hand at some even more hair-raising activities. The town of Gap is the extreme-sports capital of France – a mini New Zealand in the northern hemisphere. You can do anything there: white-water rafting, climbing, snowboarding, skate-boarding and any number of extreme games. When in Rome, I thought to myself, and I decided to try my hand at sky-diving. I realised then that I was thriving off the adrenaline these activities gave me. I had looked to replace the gap in my life that putting my partying days behind me had left, but I had done more than that. My addictive personality required an obsession; slowly but surely I was becoming addicted to the thrill, the fear and the challenges that these extreme activities presented me with.

It was like a drug, only this time it was one that wouldn't fuck me up.

ELEVEN

I CAN SEE FOR MILES

If anybody had told me a couple of years previously that the idea of being chased by a herd of angry bulls would be an experience I would put myself through for fun, I'd have told them they were fucking nuts. That's what Mike and Bean had in store for me next, and it was an indication of how much my life had changed that I simply took the whole prospect in my stride.

The long drive from Céüse to Pamplona in northern Spain was a gruelling one. We had been crowded enough in that little car beforehand, but now Kelly was with us it was almost insufferably cramped. It was a relief to get to a decent hotel in Pamplona, although I can't pretend to have been particularly enamoured by the place itself. Every year in July they have the week-long festival of San Fermin, the most famous element of which is the *Encierro*, or the Running of the Bulls. The cobbled streets of the old town are cordoned so that the route leads everyone into the main square. Competitors, all clad in white with red neckscarves and a red sash around their waist, congregate in the street, and a herd of agitated bulls are allowed to stampede behind them. The competitors run as fast as they can, avoiding if possible being speared by the bulls' sharp horns, until they reach the main arena. Once there, the fun continues as a crowd of smaller bulls, this time with corks on the pointed ends of their horns, are let into the square. It's a dangerous business. A significant number of people have died doing it, and even more have been very seriously injured, not only by the bulls themselves but by the terrifying stampede of people trying to get away from them.

We arrived there for a five-day stay, and it was fun being together with all the camera crew and production team again. Kelly got on well with everyone. Too well, perhaps – she would go out all night, doing I don't know what. There wasn't much I could do to stop her – I knew that the desire to quit drinking and the like has to come from yourself and in truth I was more worried for her safety than anything else. Pamplona is a rough city, especially around festival time when everyone is drunk, puking and fighting. I wanted none of that, so I got my head down and continued my training with Mike and Bean, while mentally preparing myself for the Running of the Bulls.

The tradition is that you stay up drinking all night before the run; the run itself is at seven in the morning. I decided to spend the night with Tim, one of Mike and Bean's friends. 'Let's party,' I told him. 'We'll have fun, meet some chicks, you can get drunk and I'll look after you.' Sounded straightforward enough. As it turned out, there were not that many foreigners in Pamplona, and the Spanish didn't speak much English. Add a load of alcohol into the mix and it soon became clear that all anyone really wanted to do was pick fights with us. So we spent the whole evening avoiding fights and trying to stay out of trouble.

As the sun started to rise, we headed back to the hotel

to get ready. Cameras are not allowed along the course, so Mike had rigged himself up with a chest cam and we had other cameras rigged up at various points along the route where they knew we would be passing – everything to make sure that there was enough footage of the new lean Jack running away from the steaming bulls, shit-scared. For insurance purposes, we had to have someone with us who was experienced at doing this, so we had this weird Scottish bloke on board who had run with the bulls fifty times or something crazy. Together we congregated in the square with this odd guy barking instructions at us, which we mostly ignored, and we waited for the event to begin.

A firecracker is set off to indicate that the bulls have been released from their housing. There is an incredible buzz among the competitors, a sense of excitement that is made keener by a sense of genuine fear. Everyone starts edging forward, walking slowly but ready to start sprinting as they know it will only be a few minutes before the bulls arrive to take them on. Gradually, though, the excitement turns into something more sinister. One person will freak out; that will send someone else off. Before you know it, a crazy mob mentality has descended on the whole crowd – everyone around me seemed to be losing it, and I found myself more terrified of my fellow competitors than I was of the beasts that were steaming down the road to do us harm.

And then the bulls arrive.

The ground is covered in piss, vomit and booze from the night before, which makes it slippery and treacherous. Add to that the fact that everyone is tripping up over each other and it makes the process of getting away from the bulls incredibly difficult. As soon as I saw the first bull I started running, but I tripped over this girl ahead of me. A bull came within spitting distance, lowering its head and aiming its gnarled horns at my body; somehow I managed to twist myself out of the way, before running as fast as I could. I thanked God for the punishing regimes Mike and Bean had put me through as I stormed away from those angry bulls and their vicious horns. I managed to get into the arena without any harm being done to me.

Once we were all there, the smaller bulls were released. I learned that bulls can't move left or right very quickly when they are running. Any number of people around me would run back in a straight line when they were charged, and invariably it ended up with them getting a thumping knock from the animals. The better tactic was to wait until they got close, then step to the side; that way I ensured I wasn't one of the people who were being literally hurled in the air. I also bore in mind that it is absolutely forbidden to try and touch the bulls in any way. One brash American ignored this and started wrestling one of the animals. He was doing quite well until a group of irate Spaniards pulled him away and beat the living shit out of him. He ended up in a far worse state than anyone who was hit by a bull.

For me, I had passed my final test with half the number of bruises that I expected.

Running with the bulls had been a blast, but Kelly and I couldn't get out of Pamplona itself fast enough – not only because we didn't care for the place, but also because tensions between me, Mike and Bean were starting to get kind of high. We had been working together for a long time, and they had been pushing me to my physical and mental limit in an effort to get me ready for

El Capitan. The climb was only three weeks away, and I had to be ready. But I was starting to get pissed off at being told what to do all the time – it wasn't something I had ever taken well to – and the strain was beginning to show. I arrived back in London with my sister, and spent a bit of time relaxing, but the time was fast approaching for us to fly out to Yosemite, and we needed to keep training.

I went down to Bristol to learn some more climbing techniques with Mike and Bean, but while we were there it was clear that the tensions between us hadn't simply evaporated by a bit of time apart. We had this big bust-up where I just snapped and started yelling abuse; we all said stuff that we didn't mean and a few things that we did. We were all at fault, but none of us could see that at the time, and I had had enough. I went upstairs, packed my bag and caught the train back to London.

For days we had no contact with each other. The producers were going nuts, wondering what was happening with the project and trying to persuade me to make it up with Mike and Bean and go ahead with the big climb. But I had had enough of doing everything on their terms, enough of them firing so many things at me that I really couldn't think straight. I'm the first to admit that when I feel crowded, physically or mentally, I get kind of pissy, and that was what was happening. I'm not a perfect human being, and the cracks were beginning to show. I didn't know if I wanted to carry on.

I had achieved enough, hadn't I? I'd gone sober, I had found a new focus, I had lost weight and become healthy. Surely I didn't need to put myself through this any more. Surely I didn't have to take this shit.

But then I thought of the heights of El Capitan. That was my real goal. Everything else had just been leading up to it. How would I feel if I gave it up now, just a couple of weeks before achieving what I had set out to do? I suddenly saw quite clearly that it was not an option. If I could get sober – the most difficult thing I've ever done – then I could cross this bridge with Mike and Bean. I realised how much I owed them, that they had given me so much in terms of friendship and support that it would be churlish of me to let my feelings get in the way. I went back down to Bristol and we talked things over, put it behind us and looked to the future. And the future held only one thing for us: El Capitan.

By the time we arrived in Yosemite, everything was cool between us. But I still didn't think I was anywhere near a competent enough climber to have a crack at El Cap. Yosemite is a *hard* place to climb. You're not climbing faces, like you are in most places; you're climbing cracks, and that is not easy. As soon as I arrived, the positive thoughts I had been thinking completely dissipated, and I started to get utterly demoralised. Life wasn't helped by the fact that the campsite at Yosemite was a total shithole – there are no showers, so you have to wash in the river, and you need to keep half an eye out for bears the whole time. It was thirty-odd degrees every day, and you get so thirsty in that kind of heat that I knew how uncomfortable the climb was going to be.

We spent several days fine-tuning our climbing skills. I was doing more and more leading, including multi-pitch routes of upwards of a thousand feet, so that I could get used to it; but more than anything else it brought home to me how under-prepared I was. Crack climbing like this was a whole other ball game, and I began to feel an inexorable tide of panic rising in my chest. How the fuck was I going to get up El Capitan?

D-day minus three. We were to climb the east

buttress as our final warm-up exercise. The east buttress is basically just an easier ascent, and quite an achievement in itself; but I had been climbing for six days solid without a rest day, and when I woke up that morning I instantly knew that my heart wasn't going to be in it. I was tired, I was unprepared, I needed more practice. But there was no time for that.

It was going to be thirty-four degrees that day, and we would be in the sun from eight in the morning until it went down. The three-man team ahead of us made good time, but I had brought extra water for us because I knew how dehydrated we were going to be, and that additional weight, together with my inexperience, slowed us down. And we still ran out of water two hours from the top. It was a fourteen-hundred-foot climb, and by the time we reached the summit, I was exhausted. We were expecting the team ahead to be there waiting for us, but we had taken far too long to make the ascent and they had left. To make matters worse, we couldn't find the east ledges. These are a series of chains for you to abseil down, and are by far the quickest route of getting back to the bottom. Miss those, and the only descent is on foot, down a ten-mile trail to base camp.

But the trail is impossible to find after dark. And night was approaching.

Mike and Paul, the other safety guy who was with us, would have to find it, but I was in no fit state to join them. They would have to leave me alone at the top while they ran off to pick up the trail.

It's a lonely place in the fading light. With only my exhaustion to keep me company, and knowing that we had to make it down to the bottom that night if we were to avoid the sub-zero temperatures that we could expect up there after dark, I fell into a crumpled heap and allowed panic to take over. My kidneys hurt through lack of water, my muscles were shrieking at me not to put them through any more punishment, and I felt my whole body shutting down in exhaustion. I wanted to be anywhere but there as I wept in fear and confusion. Night fell.

Suddenly I became aware of the fact that Mike was next to me again. He sat with me for a moment before telling me in a quiet but firm voice what we had to do. 'Jack,' he told me. 'I've found the trail. The only way we're going to get out of this all right is if we start walking now. We need to get back to base camp.'

I knew that what he was saying was right, but it took the most supreme effort of will to force my body into action. My mouth was like sandpaper through dehydration, and all around was pitch black. We fitted head torches and started slowly to pick our way through the forest, staying on the path that Mike had located.

We had been going for about two and a half hours when my vision started to blur and I could sense that my body was close to collapse. I needed a physical strength that was eluding me if I was going to make it down unharmed. And in that moment I had a flash of understanding. Since I had become sober, committed myself to twelve-step recovery and acknowledged the existence in my life of a higher power, I had been presented with a continuous set of hurdles to cross. That they were hurdles of my own making did not matter: they were there so that I could continuously affirm my commitment to the path that I had chosen for my life. And so I prayed. I prayed to the forces of nature I had chosen to be my guide to continue to help me conquer these challenges. It was the most heartfelt prayer I have ever made.

And take it for what you will, but the very moment I stopped praying, at ten o'clock at night on that dark, treacherous mountainside, a butterfly landed on my hand. I felt it flutter on my skin and took it as a sign: I'm not going to die up here; I am going to be OK.

My prayer had been answered with something very real: the ability and the need to go on.

We reached base camp two hours later. The first thing I had to do was drink water – and I did that like it was going out of fashion while Mike ranted and raved at the other team that had left us at the top. But all that stuff seemed irrelevant to me now. I went to sleep, and when I woke up I had never felt so good or so confident in my life. I had been in such a shitty situation, but by drawing on what I had learned and putting confidence in my abilities to deal with it, I had pulled through.

I felt like a different person. The big climb was two days away, and I realised that what I needed to climb the main face of El Capitan was not just technique, fitness and equipment, although they were all important. It was confidence in myself, and all of a sudden I had bucket-loads.

My new-found focus saw me through the next couple of days. We had to get everything we needed for the big climb organised: food, water, equipment. The route we had chosen is called the Salathe Wall, and for a long time it was the toughest rock climb in the world. Everything had to be just right. After the scare I had received on the practice run, however, I had a new sense of determination and a calmness that allowed me to focus on the jobs in hand.

Finally the day arrived. Everything I had been training for over the past months had been leading up to this. It was intimidating, but it felt good finally to have reached the moment where I could put all my skills and confidence to the test and, more importantly, prove myself.

I led the first pitch that took us off the ground. The Salathe Wall is a route that follows the natural cracks along the rock face, and the first day's climbing was to take us up to Heart Ledge, from where we would abseil down to the base of a separate crack that takes you up to the top. At this point we would rest for a day, then meet up with our bags and supplies, and start the main climb, which was expected to take us four to six days.

At the base I acquainted myself with a piece of equipment called a portaledge. This is an aluminium-framed canvas hammock that you attach to the rock face in the event that there is not a natural ledge to sleep on – not something to be recommended for anyone without a head for heights as there's nothing really apart from the canvas between you and thousands of feet of sheer drop. We also filled up our haul bags with the food we would need. The haul bags would be suspended on ropes below us, and we would pull them up behind us after we finished each pitch. They weighed about two hundred pounds each, and we packed enough food and water for three nights and four days, little knowing that the ascent would actually take us five nights and six days.

On the first day we didn't get as far as we intended to, the result being that on day two everybody was rushing. You can't hurry things when you're climbing a wall that size, and it was a case of more haste, less speed. In fact it was complete fucking pandemonium as everyone tried to get their shit together. We ended up having to bust a gut to make up time, and do three pitches in a single day – exhausting work for anyone, let alone me.

Even then we didn't manage to get to the ledges we were aiming for – perfect places to sleep – before nightfall. Mike and Bean elected to stay in a portaledge in a very precarious position a couple of hundred feet below; other members of the team continued the climb and fixed ropes for me to follow them. The result was that the cameraman and I were left suspended with only a two-inch ledge to stand on, cold and scared, two thousand feet off the ground with little bugs swarming around us. Thank God I had company there: we stayed like that for about four hours before we could continue the climb in the pitch black, the way lit only by our head torches. We made it in the small hours of the morning, and a rocky ledge as a bed never felt so good, even though it was only for a few short hours.

When I woke up, I wanted to be anywhere but there. 'Fuck this,' I told everyone. 'You guys are idiots. You don't even know what you're doing.' I seriously considered making my way down, which was still an option so early in the climb. It wasn't fun. I wasn't enjoying it. We were on half rations as our food supply was dwindling due to the fact that we were taking so long, and I seriously doubted that we would ever make it. But Mike and Bean persuaded me to keep it up. No one ever said it would be a laugh, they reminded me. It would only be retrospectively that I would be able to look back on the climb and revel in my achievement.

Achievement. It was what my life had started to be about. I took a deep breath, regrouped my courage and carried on.

As the climb progressed, it became more treacherous. The rock face became smoother and more difficult to scale. We reached a stage of the wall called El Cap Spire. This is a pinnacle that juts out from the face, and nobody knows exactly what is keeping it there apart from its immense weight. The tiniest earth tremor, though, and there's no doubt that it will go hurtling down to ground zero. It had been decided that I would wait there with Bean and one other member of the team, while the other, more expert, climbers went ahead and fixed ropes for us – it would be far too difficult for me to lead the way. We would then jumar up. This is a technique that uses clamps that clip on to the rope that only move in one direction. They effectively allow you to walk vertically up a rock face. But they say that one hour's jumaring is the equivalent of walking twenty miles on the flat. I had days of it ahead of me.

To make things worse, the final hurdle of climbing the Salathe Wall is a huge overhanging rock face. Get caught there in the middle of a storm and you are in mortal danger, and jumaring at that angle involves pulling your entire body weight up the rope. It took a lot of sweat, a bit of blood and quite a few tears to reach the Sloping Ledge but, once we were there, I knew there was nothing between me and the summit except a good deal of physical exertion, and I was prepared for it. We struggled on.

By the time the Sloping Ledge was complete, there was just one more section of the climb, but perhaps the most gruelling, the one where my mettle was to be genuinely tested. The Headwall overhangs at an angle of about thirty degrees. There is nothing between you and the ground, three thousand feet directly below you, and, because of the incline, the ropes that you use to climb it hang about ten feet from the wall. You are literally jumaring up through thin air. It took an hour of some of the most intense physical and mental concentration I have ever experienced, but by the time I completed it and reached what is known as the Long Ledge, we were almost there. I wish I could capture and bottle the excitement I felt once I knew the end was in sight. It was the best climb I have ever had, and I know how lucky I will be if I ever find one better. Whether it was the route itself or the fact that I knew it was almost over, I can't say; but I do know that it was the most magical, amazing feeling, topped only by the pleasure of pulling myself over the final few boulders to the top. Exhausted. Hurting. But more satisfied and complete than I had ever been.

I had done it.

I looked around me. The landscape was sparse, barren almost. Nothing to look at, really, if you weren't aware of what had just been done. But to me it was the best place in the world.

I had done it.

For the first time in my life, I had achieved what I had set out to do. I had never really pursued anything worthwhile in my life: I had dropped out of school, I had frittered my time and my health away on drugs and alcohol, I had never really *done* anything. And now this. All the strain and exertions of the past few months had been leading up to this moment, and there had been times when I thought it just wouldn't be possible, that I didn't have it in me. I had had to look deep inside, plumb depths of determination that I never knew I had.

I had done it.

It didn't seem possible. As I sat there with Mike and Bean, surveying the landscape below, I felt the emotion welling up in me.

I had done it.

We hugged, and tears filled my eyes as the full magnitude of what I had achieved hit home.

There was food waiting at the top, and we ate our fill and drank in the scenery as we came to terms with the fact that it was over. But once I was up there, I wanted to get down: my mum and dad were waiting down at the foot of the mountain by Yosemite Falls, and I was overwhelmed with a desire to see them. There was just the small matter of a nine mile hike down to the bottom the same walk I had done a few nights before, but in daylight this time – but what's that when you've just climbed El Capitan?

I saw them standing there waiting for me, pride etched on their faces like I have never seen it before. We hugged and cried. They told me how proud they were. They gazed up the rock face in comical disbelief.

We talked about the mountain. We talked about the climb. But we didn't talk about the one thing that was on all our minds. That what I had just done was more than simply climbing a mountain. It was proof positive that I had turned my life around. I had gone from being depressed, strung out, addicted to drugs and alcohol, wanting to kill myself, to becoming the man I guess I always wanted to be when I was a kid. I had put the old Jack Osbourne behind me, I had come of age, and I had shown to myself, my parents and the world that I wasn't that insecure, scared, off-the-rails kid I used to be.

I truly believed I had become a better person. And now, I had a future.

EPILOGUE

Within a few hours of completing El Capitan, I was with my parents in the most luxurious hotel I have ever stayed in, where I lounged around in a hot tub then ate my way through a fabulous dinner to replace some of the seven pounds I had lost in the past few days. And since then, my life has been a bit like that: one minute I'll be in a tent in the desert, the next I'll be drinking tea in the Dorchester. Never for one second do I forget how lucky I am.

But there are two kinds of luck. the luck that just happens, and the luck that you make for yourself. I could have just breezed through life, enjoying my privilege and never really giving myself any challenges; and maybe there would have been nothing so wrong with that. I am conscious, though, that I have been given a second chance, and this time round I know that I want more out of my life than fancy hotels and the trappings of wealth and fame. Climbing El Cap, and all that went before, showed me how fulfilling life can be, and now I'm hungry for more.

I'm not saying that I have turned into a relentless adrenaline machine, though. All work and no play would make this particular Jack a dull boy, and I see nothing wrong with enjoying to the full everything it is my good fortune to have – just so long as I can deal with the media attention that comes with it. It wasn't so long after I climbed El Cap that I found myself plastered over the papers for a very different reason – my supposed relationship with supermodel Kate Moss. Well, I guess there are worse things to have said about you, and at least this one kind of had its basis in truth.

Kate and I are good friends, and have been for the last three years or so. We hang out now and then, but there was never really any more to it than that. I was invited to celebrate her birthday at a club in Los Angeles called Teddies in January 2006, so of course I went. As the evening progressed, I found myself on the dance floor with Kate. One thing led to another, and before I knew it we were kissing. I can't deny it was a bit of an epic moment for me – there had been plenty of women before that, but this would be a feather in the cap of any young man, and I enjoyed it as much as anybody else would as my friends looked on in amusement, astonishment and perhaps a little bit of envy! A kiss, however, as the song goes, is just a kiss, and there was little more to it than that. At the end of the evening we went our separate ways, the best of friends, as ever we were.

Needless to say, the rumours didn't take very long to fly around the globe. Soon enough the old game of Chinese Whispers had run its course, and in the eyes of the media, Kate and I were an item. Like I say, not the worst rumour, but a little off the mark.

Stuff like that is all good fun, but it's only one part of my life now, and a small part at that. Since I realised what is possible if you put your mind to it, I have become pretty much addicted to pushing myself in ways I never imagined possible. In the early part of 2006 I found myself, again with Mike and Bean, deep in the heart of the Sahara desert, competing in a competition called the *Marathon des Sables*. It is one of the toughest foot races in the world, a hundred and fifty-one miles over six days through the heat of the Sahara. There was never any real chance of my being able to complete such a fiendish race – despite Mike and Bean's demanding fitness regime, I have some way to go before I am quite the calibre of athlete that can manage such extremes without damaging themselves – but I think I did myself justice in the portion of the race that I was able to finish. Failure is a big part of success, and with a good mental attitude and a lot more physical work, perhaps I'll be in good enough shape to complete the whole thing one day.

After that, my diary is one long list of the most adrenaline-packed extreme sports in the world. There's a trip to South Africa to do the world's highest bungy jump off the Bloukrans Bridge – two hundred and sixteen metres, or the equivalent of the BT Tower in London, including the antennae. There's a trip to the jungles of Belize to train with the Royal Marines, followed by a five-day trip through the jungle to find some Aztec ruins that were only discovered a couple of years ago, and which only a few people have ever seen. We're going to Japan to hang out with an order of monks from Mount Hiei. They are part of the Tendai sect of Buddhism, and they have a tradition of running a marathon a day for a hundred days in order to attain spiritual enlightenment. If you manage to run a thousand marathons in a thousand days you become a 'living god' – there is one in existence who wears glasses and smokes cigarettes! And there's a journey to New Zealand – the extreme-sports capital of the world – to do as many extreme sports as we can pack into our allotted time, including white-water kayaking over a twenty-one-foot waterfall. After that it's India, where I hope to try out some ancient Indian kushti wrestling – one of their national sports – followed by a wrestling match at a stadium with eight thousand people looking on. Then to Spain, where I'm going to learn how to sky-dive, before sky-diving back into England.

I'm not worried that I'll run out of challenges, because I can always return to my climbing, where there is always room for improvement, and always scarier, harder things to climb. That's where my passion is now, where my addiction lies – I even hope to scale Everest in the next three years.

I'll never forget, though, that I owe my new life to the principles of twelve-step recovery. Wherever I am in the world, whatever I'm doing, I do my best to attend meetings and to keep the twelve steps in the forefront of my mind. I even go out of my way to help other people who are going through the same hell that I experienced, because I know that the only way they can battle their problems is with the help and support of others who know how difficult it is. If I can be some sort of inspiration to people fighting with drug and alcohol addictions, then so much the better. I know my dad has said that the fact that I have managed to sober up and do what I have done with my life has been an inspiration to him to clean up his act once and for all. He's clean now, and has been for a couple of years: for me, that alone makes my recovery worthwhile.

Because ultimately, the most important thing in my life is my family. We've been called all the things under the sun: dysfunctional, crazy, hilarious, shocking. But at the end of the day we're just a family like any other, close-knit, loving and there for each other. It's no coincidence that Mum's illness was the catalyst for everything that followed in my life. We all live with the constant, nagging fear that her cancer will come back; I seem to spend my days trying to persuade her to slow down, to take it easy, to live a bit more healthily, because I'm terrified that if she relapses, she won't be strong enough this time round to deal with it. We're all scared that one day she will be taken from us. If that happens, God only knows what we will do. She's at the centre of everything, and if she wasn't there, the whole Osbourne family will fall apart.

It's a terrible fear. But if my experiences over the last couple of years have taught me anything, it's that you can't allow that fear to take over your life. Like El Capitan, it's there to be conquered: all it takes is willpower and the strength to succeed.

Now that I have those two things, I pray they never leave me.